Workshop on Evaluation Metrics and System Comparison for Automatic Summarization 2012

Held at the 2012 Conference of the North American Chapter of the Association for Computational Linguistics: Human Language Technologies (NAACL-HLT 2012)

Montreal, Quebec, Canada
3 – 8 June 2012

ISBN: 978-1-62276-572-0

Printed from e-media with permission by:

Curran Associates, Inc.
57 Morehouse Lane
Red Hook, NY 12571

Some format issues inherent in the e-media version may also appear in this print version.

Printed by Curran Associates, Inc. (2013)

Association for Computational Linguistics
209 N. Eighth Street
Stroudsburg, Pennsylvania 18360

Phone: 1-570-476-8006
Fax: 1-570-476-0860

acl@aclweb.org

Additional copies of this publication are available from:

Curran Associates, Inc.
57 Morehouse Lane
Red Hook, NY 12571 USA
Phone: 845-758-0400
Fax: 845-758-2634
Email: curran@proceedings.com
Web: www.proceedings.com

Introduction

Welcome to the NAACL/HLT 2012 Workshop on Evaluation Metrics and System Comparison for Automatic Summarization. One of the goals of the workshop is to give a retrospective analysis of evaluation methods employed at the Text Analysis Conferences (TAC) and its predecessor, the Document Understanding Conferences (DUC). The other goal is to set plans for the future as we introduce the new task of summarization of scientific articles.

We have planned two invited presentations. Dragomir Radev will talk about his own work on summarization of scientific articles, as well as provide us with some background on related work. Lucy Vanderwende will present the plans for the new summarization task, the evaluation and the time line for future shared tasks. We have reserved ample time for discussion.

In the six regular presentations we will discuss a range of exciting topics in summarization and evaluation. These include task-based evaluations of summarization, assessments of the accuracy of current automatic evaluations, the benefits from using several automatic evaluation measures, case studies of differences between manual and automatic evaluation, cross-lingual summarization and steps towards abstractive summarization.

We anticipate a lively and rewarding workshop. Thank you for your participation!

John M. Conroy
Hoa Trang Dang
Ani Nenkova
Karolina Owczarzak

Organizers:

John M. Conroy, IDA Center for Computing Sciences
Hoa Trang Dang, National Institute for Standards and Technology
Ani Nenkova, University of Pennsylvania
Karolina Owczarzak, National Institute for Standards and Technology

Program Committee:

Enrique Amigo (UNED, Madrid)
Giuseppe Carenini (University of British Columbia)
Katja Filippova (Google Research)
George Giannakopoulos (NCSR Demokritos)
Dan Gillick (University of California at Berkeley)
Min-Yen Kan (National University of Singapore)
Guy Lapalme (University of Montreal)
Yang Liu (University of Texas, Dallas)
Annie Louis (University of Pennsylvania)
Kathy McKeown (Columbia University)
Gabriel Murray (University of British Columbia)
Dianne O'Leary (University of Maryland)
Drago Radev (University of Michigan)
Steve Renals (University of Edinburgh)
Horacio Saggion (Universitat Pompeu Fabra)
Judith Schlesinger (IDA Center for Computing Sciences)
Josef Steinberger (European Commission Joint Research Centre)
Stan Szpakowicz (University of Ottawa)
Lucy Vanderwende (Microsoft Research)
Stephen Wan (CSIRO ICT Centre)
Xiaodan Zhu (National Research Council Canada)

Invited Speakers:

Drago Radev (University of Michigan)
Lucy Vanderwende (Microsoft Research)

Table of Contents

Conference Program

8:50AM	Opening remarks
9:00AM	*An Assessment of the Accuracy of Automatic Evaluation in Summarization* Karolina Owczarzak, John M. Conroy, Hoa Trang Dang and Ani Nenkova
9:30AM	*Using the Omega Index for Evaluating Abstractive Community Detection* Gabriel Murray, Giuseppe Carenini and Raymond Ng
10:00AM	*Machine Translation for Multilingual Summary Content Evaluation* Josef Steinberger and Marco Turchi
10:30AM	BREAK
11:00AM	A new pilot task: summarization of academic articles by Lucy Vanderwende
11:40AM	Discussion and planning for the pilot task
12:30PM	LUNCH
2:30PM	Generation of surveys of research areas by Dragomir Radev
3:30PM	BREAK
4:00PM	*Ecological Validity and the Evaluation of Speech Summarization Quality* Anthony McCallum, Cosmin Munteanu, Gerald Penn and Xiaodan Zhu
4:30PM	*The Heterogeneity Principle in Evaluation Measures for Automatic Summarization* Enrique Amigó, Julio Gonzalo and Felisa Verdejo
5:00PM	*Discrepancy Between Automatic and Manual Evaluation of Summaries* Shamima Mithun, Leila Kosseim and Prasad Perera

An Assessment of the Accuracy of Automatic Evaluation in Summarization

Karolina Owczarzak
Information Access Division
National Institute of Standards and Technology
karolina.owczarzak@gmail.com

John M. Conroy
IDA Center for Computing Sciences
conroy@super.org

Hoa Trang Dang
Information Access Division
National Institute of Standards and Technology
hoa.dang@nist.gov

Ani Nenkova
University of Pennsylvania
nenkova@seas.upenn.edu

Abstract

Automatic evaluation has greatly facilitated system development in summarization. At the same time, the use of automatic evaluation has been viewed with mistrust by many, as its accuracy and correct application are not well understood. In this paper we provide an assessment of the automatic evaluations used for multi-document summarization of news. We outline our recommendations about how any evaluation, manual or automatic, should be used to find statistically significant differences between summarization systems. We identify the reference automatic evaluation metrics—ROUGE 1 and 2—that appear to best emulate human pyramid and responsiveness scores on four years of NIST evaluations. We then demonstrate the accuracy of these metrics in reproducing human judgements about the relative content quality of pairs of systems and present an empirical assessment of the relationship between statistically significant differences between systems according to manual evaluations, and the difference according to automatic evaluations. Finally, we present a case study of how new metrics should be compared to the reference evaluation, as we search for even more accurate automatic measures.

1 Introduction

Automatic evaluation of content selection in summarization, particularly the ROUGE evaluation toolkit (Lin and Hovy, 2003), has been enthusiastically adopted by researchers since its introduction in 2003. It is now standardly used to report results in publications; however we have a poor understanding of the accuracy of automatic evaluation. How often do we publish papers where we report an improvement according to automatic evaluation, but nevertheless, a standard manual evaluation would have led us to different conclusions? In our work we directly address this question, and hope that our encouraging findings contribute to a better understanding of the strengths and shortcomings of automatic evaluation.

The aim of this paper is to give a better assessment of the automatic evaluation metrics for content selection standardly used in summarization research. We perform our analyses on data from the 2008-2011 Text Analysis Conference (TAC)[1] organized by the National Institute of Standards and Technology (NIST). We choose these datasets because in early evaluation initiatives, the protocol for manual evaluation changed from year to year in search of stable manual evaluation approaches (Over *et al.*, 2007). Since 2008, however, the same evaluation protocol has been applied by NIST assessors and we consider it to be the model that automatic metrics need to emulate.

We start our discussion by briefly presenting the manual procedure for comparing systems (Section 2) and how these scores should be best used to identify significant differences between systems over a given test set (Section 3). Then, we embark on our discussion of the accuracy of automatic evaluation and its ability to reproduce manual scoring.

To begin our analysis, we assess the accuracy of common variants of ROUGE on the TAC 2008-2011 datasets (Section 4.1). There are two aspects of evaluation that we pay special attention to:

Significant difference Ideally, all system comparisons should be performed using a test for sta-

[1] http://www.nist.gov/tac/

tistical significance. As both manual metrics and automatic metrics are noisy, a statistical hypothesis test is needed to estimate the probability that the differences observed are what would be expected if the systems are comparable in their performance. When this probability is small (by convention 0.05 or less) we reject the null hypothesis that the systems' performance is comparable.

It is important to know if scoring a system via an automatic metric will lead to conclusions about the relative merits of two systems different from what one would have concluded on the basis of manual evaluation. We report very encouraging results, showing that automatic metrics rarely contradict manual metrics, and some metrics never lead to contradictions. For completeness, given that most papers do not report significance, we also compare the agreement between manual and automatic metrics without taking significance into account.

Type of comparison Established manual evaluations have two highly desirable properties: (1) they can tell apart good automatic systems from bad automatic systems and (2) they can differentiate automatic summaries from those produced by humans with high accuracy. Both properties are essential. Obviously, choosing the better system in development cycles is key in eventually improving overall performance. Being able to distinguish automatic from manual summaries is a general sanity test [2] that any evaluation adopted for wide use is expected to pass—it is useless to report system improvements when it appears that automatic methods are as good as human performance[3]. As we will see, there is no single ROUGE variant that has both of these desirable properties.

Finally, in Section 5, we discuss ways to compare other automatic evaluation protocols with the reference ROUGE metrics we have established. We define standard tests for significance that would identify evaluations that are significantly more accurate than the current reference measures, thus warranting wider adoption for future system development and reporting of results. As a case study we apply these to the TAC AESOP (Automatically Evaluating Summaries of Peers) task which called for the development of novel evaluation techniques that are more accurate than ROUGE evaluations.

2 Manual evaluation

Before automatic evaluation methods are developed, it is necessary to establish a desirable manual evaluation which the automatic methods will need to reproduce. The type of summarization task must also be precisely specified—single- or multi-document summarization, summarization of news, meetings, academic articles, etc. Saying that an automatic evaluation correlates highly with human judgement in general, is disturbingly incomplete, as the same automatic metric can predict some manual evaluation scores for some summarization tasks well, while giving poor correlation with other manual scores for certain tasks (Lin, 2004; Liu and Liu, 2010).

In our work, we compare automatic metrics with the manual methods used at TAC: Pyramid and Responsiveness. These manual metrics primarily aim to assess if the content of the summary is appropriately chosen to include only important information. They do not deal directly with the linguistic quality of the summary—how grammatical are the sentences or how well the information in the summary is organized. Subsequently, in the experiments that we present in later sections, we do not address the assessment of automatic evaluations of linguistic quality (Pitler *et al.*, 2010), but instead analyze the performance of ROUGE and other related metrics that aim to score summary content.

The Pyramid evaluation (Nenkova *et al.*, 2007) relies on multiple human-written gold-standard summaries for the input. Annotators manually identify shared content across the gold-standards regardless of the specific phrasing used in each. The pyramid score is based on the "popularity" of information in the gold-standards. Information that is shared

[2]For now, automatic systems do not have the performance of humans, thus, the ability to distinguish between human and automatically generated summaries is an exemplar of the wider problem of distinguishing high quality summaries from others.

[3]Such anomalous findings, when using automatic evaluation, have been reported for some summarization genres such as summarization of meetings (Galley, 2006).

across several human gold-standards is given higher weight when a summary is evaluated relative to the gold-standard. Each evaluated summary is assigned a score which indicates what fraction of the most important information for a given summary size is expressed in the summary, where importance is determined by the overlap in content across the human gold-standards.

The Responsiveness metric is defined for query-focused summarization, where the user's information need is clearly stated in a short paragraph. In this situation, the human assessors are presented with the user query and a summary, and are asked to assign a score that reflects to what extent the summary satisfies the user's information need. There are no human gold-standards, and the linguistic quality of the summary is to some extent incorporated in the score, because information that is presented in a confusing manner may not be seen as relevant, while it could be interpreted by the assessor more easily in the presence of a human gold-standard. Given that all standard automatic evaluation procedures compare a summary with a set of human gold-standards, it is reasonable to expect that they will be more accurate in reproducing results from Pyramid evaluation than results from Responsiveness judgements.

3 Comparing systems

Evaluation metrics are used to determine the relative quality of a summarization system *in comparison* to one or more systems, which is either another automatic summarizer, or a human reference summarizer. Any evaluation procedure assigns a score to each summary. To identify which of the two systems is better, we could simply average the scores of summaries produced by each system in the test set, and compare these averages. This approach is straightforward; however, it gives no indication of the statistical significance of the difference between the systems. In system development, engineers may be willing to adopt new changes only if they lead to significantly better performance that cannot be attributed to chance.

Therefore, in order to define more precisely what it means for a summarization system to be "better" than another for a given evaluation, we employ statistical hypothesis testing comparisons of summarization systems on the same set of documents. Given an evaluation of two summarization systems A and B we have the following:

Definition 1. *We say a summarizer A "significantly outperforms" summarizer B for a given evaluation score if the null hypothesis of the following paired test is rejected with 95% confidence.*

> *Given two vectors of evaluation scores x and y, sampled from the corresponding random variables X and Y, measuring the quality of summarizer A and B, respectively, on the same collection of document sets, with the median of x greater than the median of y,*

H_0 : *The median of $X - Y$ is 0.*

H_a : *The median of $X - Y$ is not 0.*

We apply this test using human evaluation metrics, such as pyramid and responsiveness, as well as automatic metrics. Thus, when comparing two summarization systems we can, for example, say system A significantly outperforms system B in responsiveness if the null hypothesis can be rejected. If the null hypothesis cannot be rejected, we say system *A does not significantly perform differently than* system B.

A complicating factor when the differences between systems are tested for significance, is that some inputs are simply much harder to summarize than others, and there is much variation in scores that is not due to properties of the summarizers that produced the summaries but rather properties of the input text that are summarized (Nenkova, 2005; Nenkova and Louis, 2008).

Given this variation in the data, the most appropriate approach to assess significance in the difference between system is to use *paired* rank tests such as a paired Wilcoxon rank-sum test, which is equivalent to the Mann-Whitney U test. In these tests, the scores of the two systems are compared only *for the same input* and ranks are used instead of the actual difference in scores assigned by the evaluation procedures. Prior studies have shown that paired tests for significance are indeed able to discover considerably more significant differences between systems than non-paired tests, in which the noise of input difficulty obscures the actual difference in system performance (Rankel *et al.*, 2011). For this paper, we perform all testing using the Wilcoxon sign rank test.

4 How do we identify a good metric?

If we treat manual evaluation metrics as our gold standard, then we require that a good automatic metric mirrors the distinctions made by such a manual metric. An automatic metric for summarization evaluation should reliably predict how well a summarization system would perform relative to other summarizers if a human evaluation were performed on the summaries. An automatic metric would hope to answer the question:

> Would summarizer A *significantly outperform* summarizer B when evaluated by a human?

We address this question by evaluating how well an automatic metric agrees with a human metric in its judgements in the following cases:

- all comparisons between different summarization systems
- all comparisons between systems and human summarizers.

Depending on the application, we may record the counts of agreements and disagreements or we may normalize these counts to estimate the probability that an automatic evaluation metric will agree with a human evaluation metric.

4.1 Which is the best ROUGE variant

In this section, we set out to identify which of the most widely-used versions of ROUGE have highest accuracy in reproducing human judgements about the relative merits of pairs of systems. We examine ROUGE-1, ROUGE-2 and ROUGE-SU4. For all experiments we use stemming and for each version we test scores produced both with and without removing stopwords. This corresponds to six different versions of ROUGE that we examine in detail.

ROUGE outputs several scores including precision, recall, and an F-measure. However, the most informative score appears to be recall as reported when ROUGE was first introduced (Lin and Hovy, 2003). Given that in the data we work with, summaries are produced for a specified length in words (and all summaries are truncated to the predefined length), recall on the task does not allow for artificially high scores which would result by producing a summary of excessive length.

The goal of our analysis is to identify which of the ROUGE variants is most accurate in correctly predicting which of two participating systems is the better one according to the manual pyramid and responsiveness scores. We use the data for topic-focused summarization from the TAC summarization track in 2008-2011[4].

Table 1 gives the overview of the 2008-2011 TAC Summarization data, including the number of topics and participants. For each topic there were four reference (model) summaries, written by one of the eight assessors; as a result, there were eight human "summarizers," but each produced summaries only for half of the topics.

year	topics	automatic summarizers	human summarizers	references/ topic
2008	48	58	8	4
2009	44	55	8	4
2010	46	43	8	4
2011	44	50	8	4

Table 1: Data in TAC 2008-2011 Summarization track.

We compare each pair of participating systems based on the manual evaluation score. For each pair, we are interested in identifying the system that is better. We consider both the case when an appropriate test for statistical significance has been applied to pick out the better system as well as the case where simply the average scores of systems over the test set are compared. The latter use of evaluations is most common in research papers on summarization; however, in summarization system development, testing for significance is important because a difference in summarizer scores that is statistically significant is much more likely to reflect a true difference in quality between the two systems.

Therefore, we look at agreement between ROUGE and manual metrics in two ways:

- agreement about significant differences between summarizers, according to a paired

[4] In all these years systems also competed on producing update summaries. We do not report results on this task for the sake of simplifying the discussion.

	Auto only						Human-Automatic					
	Pyr			Resp			Pyr			Resp		
	diff	no diff	contr	diff	no diff	contr	diff	no diff	contr	diff	no diff	contr
r1m	91	59	0.85	87	51	1.34	91	75	0.06	91	100	0.45
r1ms	90	59	0.83	84	50	3.01	91	75	0.06	90	100	0.45
r2m	91	68	0.19	88	60	0.47	75	75	0.62	75	100	1.02
r2ms	88	72	0	84	62	0.65	73	75	1.56	72	100	1.95
r4m	91	64	0.62	87	56	0.91	82	75	0.43	82	100	0.83
r4ms	90	64	0.04	85	55	1.15	83	75	0.81	83	100	1.20

Table 2: Average percentage agreement between ROUGE and manual metrics about significant differences on TAC 2008-2011 data. *r1* = ROUGE-1, *r2* = ROUGE-2, *r4* = ROUGE-SU4, *m* = stemmed, *s* = stopwords removed; *diff* = agreement on significant differences, *no diff* = agreement on lack of significant differences, *contr* = contradictions.

	Auto only				Human-Automatic			
	Pyr		Resp		Pyr		Resp	
metric	sig	all	sig	all	sig	all	sig	all
r1m	77	87	70	82	90	99	90	99
r1ms	77	88	69	80	90	98	90	98
r2m	81	89	75	83	75	94	75	94
r2ms	81	89	74	81	72	93	72	93
r4m	80	88	73	82	82	96	82	96
r4ms	79	89	71	81	83	96	83	96

Table 3: Average agreement between ROUGE and manual metrics on TAC 2008-2011 data. *r1* = ROUGE-1, *r2* = ROUGE-2, *r4* = ROUGE-SU4, *m* = stemmed, *s* = stopwords removed; *sig* = agreement on significant differences, *all* = agreement on all differences.

Wilcoxon test. No adjustments for multiple comparisons are made.

- agreement about any differences between summarizers (whether significant on not).

Agreements occur when the two evaluation metrics make the same distinction between System A and System B: A is significantly better than B, A is significantly worse than B, or A and B are not significantly different from each other. *Contradictions* occur when both metrics find a significant difference between A and B, but in opposite directions; this is a much more serious case than a mere lack of agreement (i.e., when one metric says A and B are not significantly different, and the other metric finds a significant difference).

Table 2 shows the average percentage agreement between ROUGE and Pyramid/Responsiveness when it comes to identifying significant differences or lack thereof. Column *diff* shows the recall of significant differences between pairs of systems (i.e., how many significant differences determined by Pyramid/Responsiveness are found by ROUGE); column *no diff* gives the recall of the cases where there are no significant differences between two systems according to Pyramid/Responsiveness.

There are a few instances of contradictions, as well, but their numbers are fairly small. "Auto only" refers to comparisons between automatic summarizers only; "Human-Automatic" refers to cases when a human summarizer is compared to an automatic summarizer. There are fewer human summarizers, so there are fewer "Human-Automatic" comparisons than "Auto only" ones.

There are a few exceptional cases where the human summarizer is not significantly better than the automatic summarizers, even according to the manual evaluation, which accounts for the uniform values in the "no difference" column (this is probably because the comparison is performed for much fewer test inputs).

Table 3 combines the number of agreements in the "difference" and "no difference" columns from Table 2 into the *sig* column, which shows accuracy: in checking system pairs for significant differences, in how many cases does ROUGE make the same decision as the manual metric (there is/isn't a significant difference between A and B). Table 3 also gives the number of agreements about *any* differences between systems, not only those that reached statistical significance; in other words, agreements on system pairwise rankings. In both tables we see that removing stopwords often decreases performance of ROUGE, although not always. Also, there is no clear winner in the ROUGE comparison: while ROUGE-2 with stemming is the best at distinguishing among automatic summarizers, ROUGE-1 is the most accurate when it comes to human–automatic comparisons. To reflect this, we adopt both ROUGE-1 and ROUGE-2 (with stemming, without removing stopwords) as our reference automatic metrics for further comparisons.

Reporting pairwise accuracy of automatic evaluation measures has several advantages over reporting correlations between manual and automatic metrics. In correlation analysis, we cannot obtain any sense of how accurate the measure is in identifying statistically significant differences. In addition, pairwise accuracy is more interpretable than correlations and gives some provisional indication about how likely it is that we are drawing a wrong conclusion when relying on automatic metric to report results.

Table 3 tells us that when statistical significance is not taken into account, in 89% of cases ROUGE-2 scores will lead to the same conclusion about the relative merits of systems as the expensive Pyramid evaluation. In 83% of cases the conclusions will agree with the Responsiveness evaluation. The accuracy of identifying significant differences is worse, dropping by about 10% for both Pyramid and Responsiveness.

Finally, we would like to get empirical estimates of the relationship between the size of the difference in ROUGE-2 scores between two systems and the agreement between manual and ROUGE-2 evaluation. The goal is to check if it is the case that if one system scores higher than another by x ROUGE points, then it would be safe to assume that a manual evaluation would have led to the same conclusion.

Figure 1 shows a histogram of differences in ROUGE-2 scores. The pairs for which this difference was significant are given in red and for those where the difference is not significant are given in blue. The histogram clearly shows that in general, the size of improvement cannot be used to replace a test for significance. Even for small differences in ROUGE score (up to 0.007) there are about 15 pairs out of 200 for which the difference is in fact significant according to Pyramid or Responsiveness. As the difference in ROUGE-2 scores between the two systems increases, there are more significant differences. For differences greater than 0.05, all differences are significant.

Figure 2 shows the histograms of differences in ROUGE-2 scores, split into cases where the pairwise ranking of systems according to ROUGE agrees with manual evaluation (blue) and disagrees (red). For score differences smaller than 0.013, about half of the times ROUGE-2 would be wrong in identifying which system in the pair is the better one according to manual evaluations. For larger differences the number of disagreements drops sharply. For this dataset, a difference in ROUGE-2 scores of more than 0.04 always corresponds to an improvement in the same direction according to the manual metrics.

5 Looking for better metrics

In the preceding sections, we established that ROUGE-2 is the best ROUGE variant for comparing two automatic systems, and ROUGE-1 is best in distinguishing between humans and machines. Obviously, it is of great interest to develop even better automatic evaluations. In this section, we outline a simple procedure for deciding if a new automatic evaluation is significantly better than a reference measure. For this purpose, we consider the automatic metrics from the TAC 2011 AESOP task, which called for the development of better automatic metrics for summarization evaluation NIST (2011).

For each automatic evaluation metric, we estimate the probability that it agrees with Pyramid or Responsiveness. Figure 3 gives the estimated probability of agreement with Pyramid and Overall Responsiveness for all AESOP 2011 metrics with an agreement of 0.6 or more. The metrics are plotted with error bars giving the 95% confidence intervals for the probability of agreement with the manual evaluations. The red-dashed line is the performance of the reference automatic evaluation, which is ROUGE-2 for machine only and ROUGE-1 for comparing machines and human summarizers. Metrics whose 95% confidence interval is below this line are significantly worse (as measured by the z-test approximation of a binomial test) than the baseline. Conversely, those whose 95% confidence interval is above the red line are significantly better than the baseline. Thus, just ROUGE-

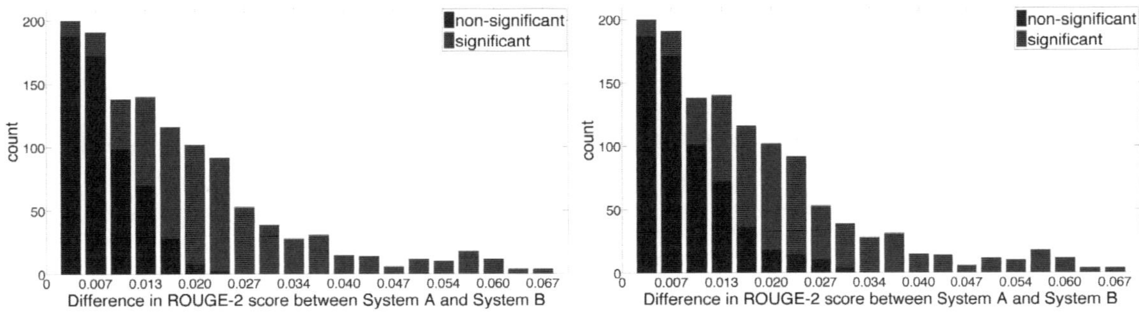

Figure 1: Histogram of the differences in ROUGE-2 score versus significant differences as determined by Pyramid (left) or Responsiveness (right).

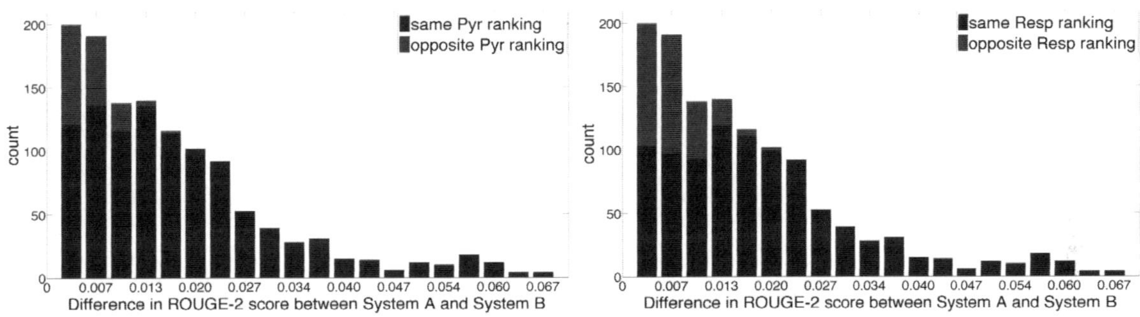

Figure 2: Histogram of the differences in ROUGE-2 score versus differences as determined by Pyramid (left) or Responsiveness (right).

BE (the MINIPAR variant of ROUGE-BE), one of NIST's baselines for AESOP, significantly outperformed ROUGE-2 for predicting pyramid comparisons; and 4 metrics: ROUGE-BE, DemokritosGR2, catholicasc1, and CLASSY1, all significantly outperform ROUGE-2 for predictiong responsiveness comparisons. Descriptions of these metrics as well as the other proposed metrics can be found in the TAC 2011 proceedings (NIST, 2011).

Similarly, Figure 4 gives the estimated probability when the comparison is made between human and machine summarizers. Here, 10 metrics are significantly better than ROUGE-1 in predicting comparisons between automatic summarization systems and human summarizers in both pyramid and responsiveness. The ROUGE-SU4 and ROUGE-BE baselines are not shown here but their performance was approximately 57% and 46% respectively.

If we limit the comparisons to only those where a significant difference was measured by Pyramid and also Overall Responsiveness, we get the plots given in Figure 5 for comparing automatic summarization systems. (The corresponding plot for comparisons between machines and humans is omitted as all differences are significant.) The results show that there are 6 metrics that are significantly better than ROUGE-2 for correctly predicting when a significant difference in pyramid scores occurs, and 3 metrics that are significantly better than ROUGE-2 for correctly predicting when a significant difference in responsiveness occurs.

6 Discussion

In this paper we provided a thorough assessment of automatic evaluation in summarization of news. We specifically aimed to identify the best variant of ROUGE on several years of TAC data and discovered that ROUGE-2 recall with stemming and stopwords not removed, provides the best agreement with manual evaluations. The results shed positive light on the automatic evaluation, as we find that ROUGE-2 agrees with manual evaluation in almost 90% of the case when statistical significance is not computed, and about 80% when it is. However, these numbers are computed in a situation where many very different systems are compared—some

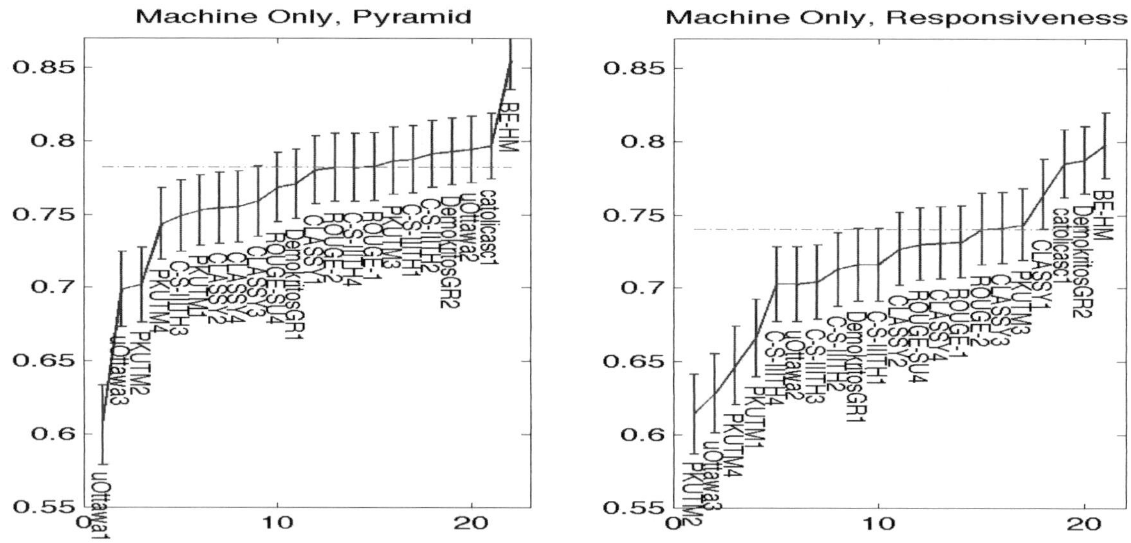

Figure 3: Pyramid and Responsiveness Agreement of AESOP 2011 Metrics for automatic summarizers.

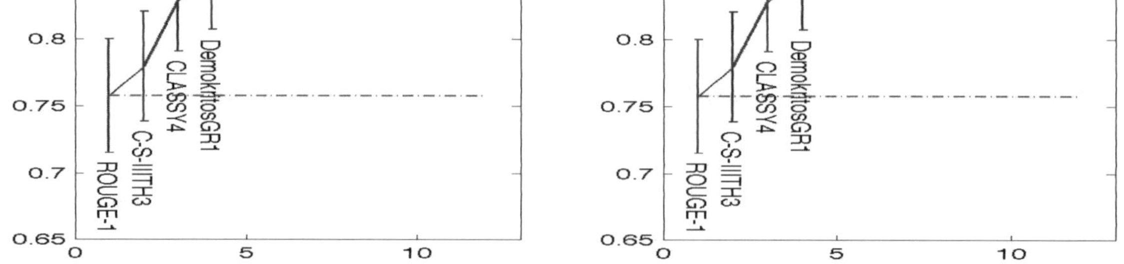

Figure 4: Pyramid and Responsiveness Significant Difference Agreement of AESOP 2011 Metrics for all summarizers.

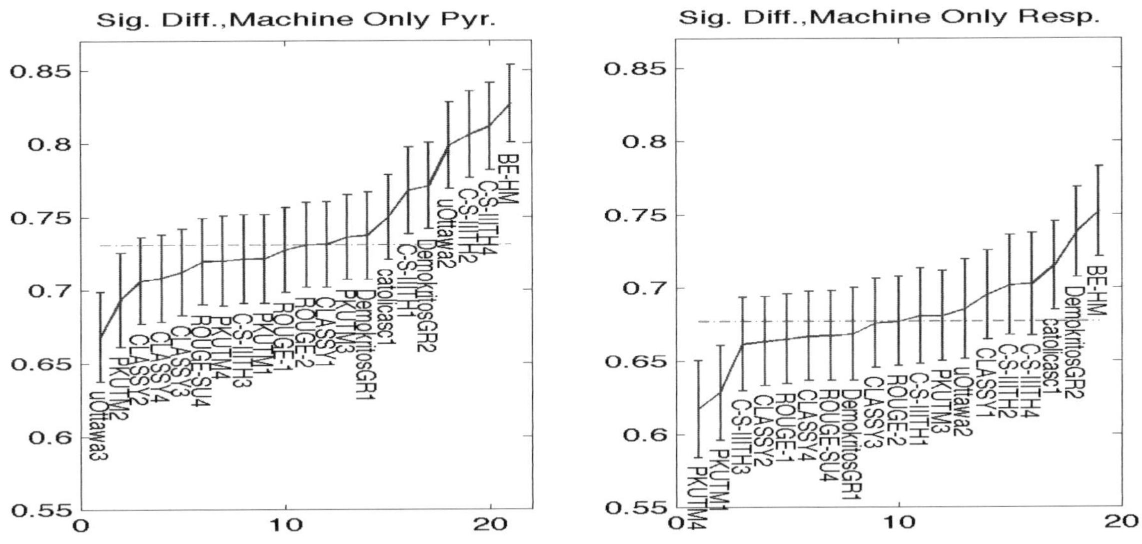

Figure 5: Pyramid and Responsiveness Significant Difference Agreement of AESOP 2011 Metrics for automatic summarizers.

very good, others bad. We examine the size of difference in ROUGE score and identify that for differences less than 0.013 a large fraction of the conclusions drawn by automatic evaluation will contradict the conclusion drawn by a manual evaluation. Future studies should be more mindful of these findings when reporting results.

Finally, we compare several alternative automatic evaluation measures with the reference ROUGE variants. We discover that many new proposals are better than ROUGE in distinguishing human summaries from machine summaries, but most are the same or worse in evaluating systems. The Basic Elements evaluation (ROUGE-BE) appears to be the strongest contender for an automatic evaluation to augment or replace the current reference.

References

Paul Over and Hoa Dang and Donna Harman. 2007. DUC in context. *Inf. Process. Manage. 43(6)*, 1506–1520.

Chin-Yew Lin and Eduard H. Hovy. 2003. Automatic Evaluation of Summaries Using N-gram Co-occurrence Statistics. *Proceeding of HLT-NAACL.*

Michel Galley. 2006. A Skip-Chain Conditional Random Field for Ranking Meeting Utterances by Importance. *Proceeding of EMNLP*, 364–372.

Feifan Liu and Yang Liu. 2010. Exploring correlation between ROUGE and human evaluation on meeting summaries. *Trans. Audio, Speech and Lang. Proc.*, 187–196.

C.Y. Lin. 2004. Looking for a Few Good Metrics: Automatic Summarization Evaluation - How Many Samples are Enough? *Proceedings of the NTCIR Workshop 4.*

Ani Nenkova and Rebecca J. Passonneau and Kathleen McKeown. 2007. The Pyramid Method: Incorporating human content selection variation in summarization evaluation. *TSLP 4(2).*

Emily Pitler and Annie Louis and Ani Nenkova. 2010. Automatic Evaluation of Linguistic Quality in Multi-Document Summarization. *Proceedings of ACL*, 544–554.

Ani Nenkova. 2005. Automatic Text Summarization of Newswire: Lessons Learned from the Document Understanding Conference. *AAAI*, 1436–1441.

Ani Nenkova and Annie Louis. 2008. Can You Summarize This? Identifying Correlates of Input Difficulty for Multi-Document Summarization. *ACL*, 825–833.

Peter Rankel and John M. Conroy and Eric Slud and Dianne P. O'Leary. 2011. Ranking Human and Machine Summarization Systems. *Proceedings of EMNLP*, 467–473.

National Institute of Standards and Technology. 2011. Text Analysis Workshop Proceedings http://www.nist.gov/tac/publications/index.html.

Using the Omega Index for Evaluating Abstractive Community Detection

Gabriel Murray
Computer Information Systems
University of the Fraser Valley
gabriel.murray@ufv.ca

Giuseppe Carenini
Computer Science
University of British Columbia
carenini@cs.ubc.ca

Raymond Ng
Computer Science
University of British Columbia
rng@cs.ubc.ca

Abstract

Numerous NLP tasks rely on clustering or community detection algorithms. For many of these tasks, the solutions are disjoint, and the relevant evaluation metrics assume non-overlapping clusters. In contrast, the relatively recent task of *abstractive community detection* (ACD) results in overlapping clusters of sentences. ACD is a sub-task of an abstractive summarization system and represents a two-step process. In the first step, we classify sentence pairs according to whether the sentences should be realized by a common abstractive sentence. This results in an undirected graph with sentences as nodes and predicted abstractive links as edges. The second step is to identify communities within the graph, where each community corresponds to an abstractive sentence to be generated. In this paper, we describe how the Omega Index, a metric for comparing non-disjoint clustering solutions, can be used as a summarization evaluation metric for this task. We use the Omega Index to compare and contrast several community detection algorithms.

1 Introduction

Automatic summarization has long been proposed as a helpful tool for managing the massive amounts of language data in our modern lives (Luhn, 1958; Edmundson, 1969; Teufel and Moens, 1997; Carbonell and Goldstein, 1998; Radev et al., 2001). Most summarization systems are *extractive*, meaning that a subset of sentences from an input document forms a summary of the whole. Particular significance may be attached to the chosen sentences, e.g. that they are relevant to a provided query, generally important for understanding the overall document, or represent a particular phenomenon such as action items from a meeting. In any case, extraction consists of binary classification of candidate sentences, plus post-processing steps such as sentence ranking and compression. In contrast, recent work attempts to replicate the *abstractive* nature of human-authored summaries, wherein new sentences are generated that describe the input document from a higher-level perspective. While some abstractive summary sentences are very similar to individual sentences from the document, others are created by synthesizing multiple document sentences into a novel abstract sentence. In this paper, we address a component of this latter task, namely identifying which sentences from the source documents should be combined in generated abstract sentences. We call this task *abstractive community detection* (ACD), and apply the task to a publicly available meeting dataset.

Herein we focus on describing how the Omega Index (Collins and Dent, 1988), a metric for comparing non-disjoint clustering solutions, can be used as a summarization evaluation metric for the ACD task. Metrics such as the Rand Index (Rand, 1971) are insufficient since they are intended only for disjoint clusters.

ACD itself is carried out in two steps. First, we classify sentence pairs according to whether they should be realized by a common abstractive sentence. For this step, we use supervised machine learning that exploits human-annotated links between abstracts and extracts for a given document. This results in an undirected graph with nodes representing sentences and edges representing predicted abstractive links. Second, we identify communities within the graph, where each community corresponds to an abstractive sentence to be generated. We experiment with several divisive community detection algorithms, and highlight the importance of selecting an algorithm that allows overlapping communities, owing to the fact that a document sentence can be expressed by, and linked to, more than one abstract summary sentence in the gold-standard.

The structure of the paper is as follow. In Section 2, we compare and contrast ACD with other relevant tasks such as extractive summarization and topic clustering. In Sections 3-4, we describe the two ACD steps before we can fully discuss evaluation methods. Section 5 describes the experimental setup and corpora used, including a description of the abstractive and extractive summary annotations and the links between them. In Section 6, we give a detailed description of the Omega Index and explain how it differs from the more common Rand Index. In Sections 7-8 we present results and draw conclusions.

2 Related Work

The ACD task differs from more common extractive summarization (Mani, 2001a; Jurafsky and Martin, 2008). Whereas extraction involves simply classifying sentences as important or not, ACD is a sub-task of *abstractive* summarization wherein document sentences are grouped according to whether they can be jointly realized by a common abstractive sentence. The first step of ACD, where we predict links between sentence pairs, can be seen to encompass extraction since the link is via an as-yet-ungenerated abstract sentence, i.e. each linked sentence is considered summary-worthy. However, the second step moves away from extraction by clustering the linked sentences from the document in order to generate abstract summary sentences.

ACD also differs from topic clustering (Malioutov and Barzilay, 2006; Joty et al., 2010), though there are superficial similarities. A first observation is that topic links and abstract links are genuinely different phenomena, though sometimes related. A single abstract sentence can reference more than one topic, e.g. *They talked about the interface design and the budget report*, and a single topic can be referenced in numerous abstract sentences. From a practical standpoint, in our work on ACD we cannot use many of the methods and evaluation metrics designed for topic clustering, due to the fact that a document sentence can belong to more than one abstract sentence. This leads to overlapping communities, whereas most work on topic clustering has focused primarily on disjoint communities where a sentence belongs to a single topic. In Section 4, we discuss community detection algorithms and evaluation metrics that allow overlapping communities.

Work on detecting *adjacency pairs* (Shriberg et al., 2004; Galley et al., 2004) also involves classifying sentence pairs as being somehow related. For example, if sentence B directly follows sentence A, we might determine that they have a relationship such as question-answer or request-accept. In contrast, with ACD there is no requirement that sentence pairs be adjacent or even in proximity to one another, nor must they be in a rhetorical relation.

Work on *sentence fusion* (Barzilay and McKeown, 2005) identifies sentences containing similar or repeated information and combines them into new sentences. In contrast, in our task sentences need not contain repeated information in order to be linked. For example, two sentences could be linked to a common abstract sentence due to a more complex rhetorical relationship such as proposal-reject or question-answer.

ACD is a more general problem that may incorporate elements of topic clustering, adjacency pair detection and other sentence clustering or pairing tasks. Here we try to directly learn the abstractive sentence links using lower-level features such as shared n-grams and cosine similarity, as described in Section 3, but in future work we will model higher-level features of topics and rhetorical structure.

3 Step 1: Building a Sentence Pair Graph

In order to describe the use of the Omega Index for the ACD task, we must first introduce the ACD task in some detail. The first step in ACD is to determine which sentence pairs are linked. If two sentences are linked, it means they can be at least partly realized in the abstract summary by a common sentence. A document sentence may "belong" to more than one abstract sentence. We take a supervised classification approach to this problem, training on a dataset containing explicit links between extract sentences and abstract sentences. The corpus and relevant annotation are described in detail in Section 5. For

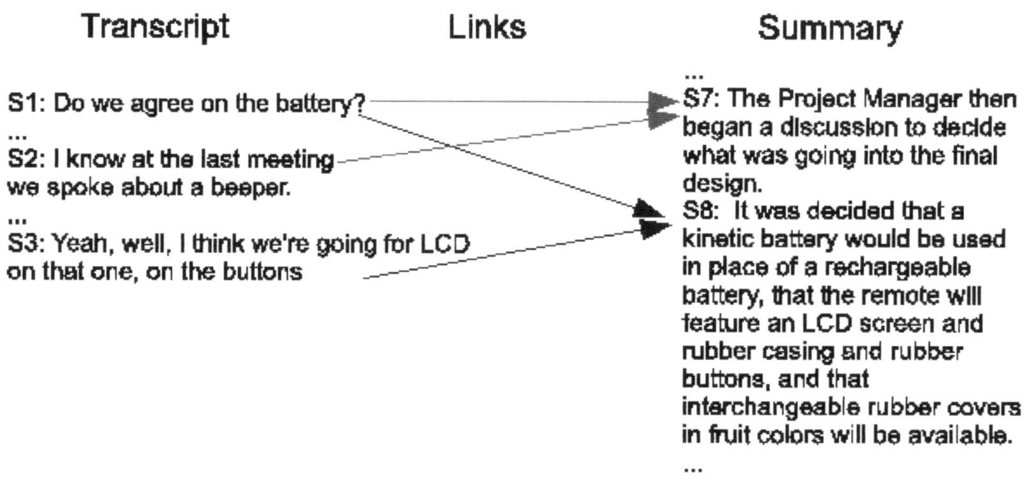

Figure 1: Linked Sentences

our gold-standard data, a sentence pair is considered linked if both sentences are linked to a common abstract sentence and not-linked otherwise.

Figure 1 shows an example snippet of linked sentences from our corpus. The first and second sentences are linked via one abstract sentence while the first and third sentences are linked via a different abstract sentence. While it is not shown in this example, note that two sentences can also be linked via more than one abstract sentence.

We take a supervised machine learning approach toward predicting whether a sentence pair is linked. For each pair, we extract features that can be classed as follows:

- **Structural:** The *intervening number* of sentences, the *document position* as indicated by the midpoint of the two sentences, the *combined length* and the *difference in length* between the two sentences, and whether the two sentences share the *same speaker*.
- **Linguistic:** The number of *shared bigrams*, *shared part-of-speech tags*, the *sum and average of tf.idf weights*, and the *cosine similarity* of the sentence vectors.

We run the trained classifier over sentence pairs, predicting abstractive links between sentences in the document. This results in an unweighted, undirected graph where nodes represent sentences and edges represent an abstractive link. Continuing with the conversation snippet from Figure 1, we would end up with a graph like Figure 2. This very simple example of a graph shows that there are abstractive links predicted between sentences s1 and s2 and between sentences s1 and s3. There is no direct link predicted between sentences s2 and s3. However, it is possible for two sentences with no predicted link between them to wind up in the same abstractive community after running a community detection algorithm on the graph. We discuss this community detection step in the following section.

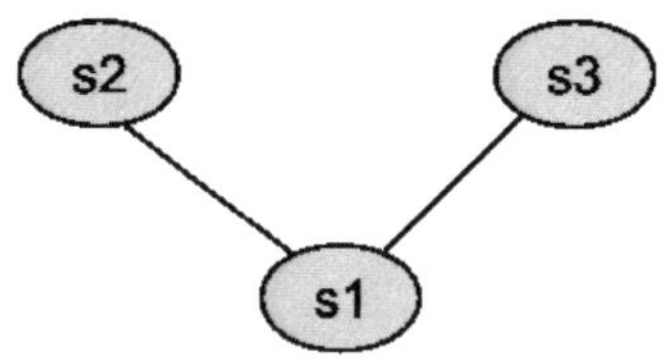

Figure 2: Graph with Sentence Nodes

4 Step 2: Discovering Abstractive Sentence Communities

In the first step of ACD, we predicted whether pairs of sentences can be at least partly realized by a common abstractive sentence. We then want to identify *communities* or clusters within the graph. Each of these communities will correspond to an abstractive

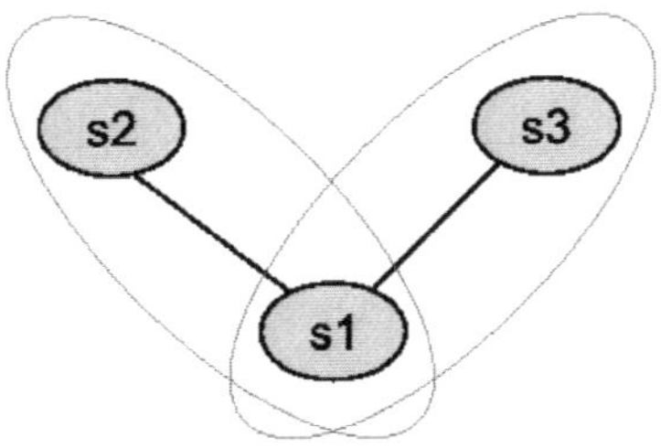

Figure 3: Overlapping Communities in Graph

sentence that we will generate. Continuing with our simple example, Figure 3 shows two communities that have been identified in the graph. Note that the communities are overlapping, as each contains sentence s1; we would generate one abstractive sentence describing sentences s1 and s2 and another describing sentences s1 and s3. We will return to this critical issue of overlapping communities shortly.

The task of identifying communities in networks or graphs has received considerable attention (Porter et al., 2009). The Girvan-Newman algorithm (Girvan and Newman, 2002) is a popular community detection method based on a measure of *betweenness*. The betweenness score for an edge is the number of shortest paths between pairs of nodes in the graph that run along that edge. An edge with a high betweenness score is likely to be between two communities and is therefore a good candidate for removal, as the goal is to break the initial graph into distinct communities. The Girvan-Newman algorithm proceeds as follows:

1. Calculate the betweenness of each edge in the graph.
2. Remove the edge with the highest betweenness.
3. For any edge affected by Step 2, recalculate betweenness.
4. Repeat steps 2 and 3 until no edges remain

In this way we proceed from the full graph with all edges intact to the point where no edges remain and each node is in its own community. The intermediate steps can be visualized by the resulting dendrogram, such as seen in Figure 4 [1].

The top row, the "leaves" of the dendrogram, represents the individual nodes in the graph. The rest of the dendrogram shows how these nodes are situated in nested communities, e.g. *b* and *c* form a community *bc* that combines with *def* to form *bcdef*. In our case, where nodes are sentences, the dendrogram shows us how sentences combine into nested communities. This can be useful for generating abstracts of different granularities, e.g. we could describe *bcdef* in one sentence or generate two sentences to separately describe *bc* and *def*.

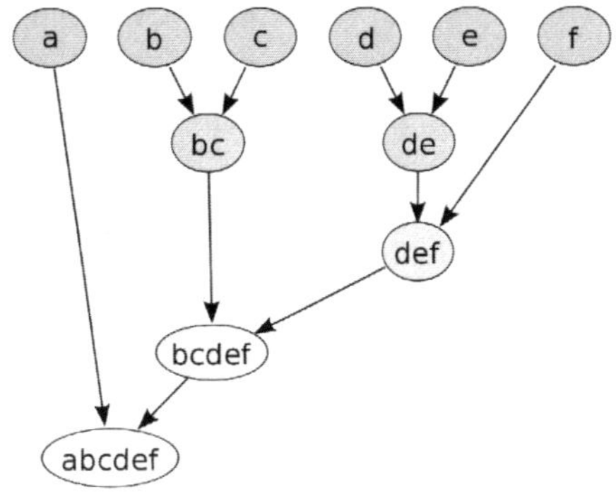

Figure 4: Community Dendrogram

The drawback of Girvan-Newman for our purposes is that it does not allow overlapping communities, and we know that our human-annotated data contain overlaps. Note from Figure 4 that all communities decompose into disjoint nested communities, such as *bcdef* being comprised of *bc* and *def*, not *bc* and *bdef* or some other overlapping case. We therefore hypothesize that Girvan-Newman in its traditional form is not sufficient for our current research. For the same reason, recent graph-based approaches to topic clustering (Malioutov and Barzilay, 2006; Joty et al., 2010) are not directly applicable here.

It is only in recent years that much attention has been paid to the problem of overlapping (or non-disjoint) communities. Here we consider two recent modifications to the Girvan-Newman algorithm that allow for overlaps. The CONGA algorithm (Gregory, 2007) extends Girvan-Newman so that instead of removing an edge on each iteration, we either remove an edge or copy a node. When a node is copied, an overlap is created. Nodes are associated with a betweenness score (called the *split betweenness*) derived from the edge betweenness scores, and at each step we either remove the edge with the highest betweenness score or copy the node with the

[1] Image Source: Wikimedia Commons (Mhbrugman)

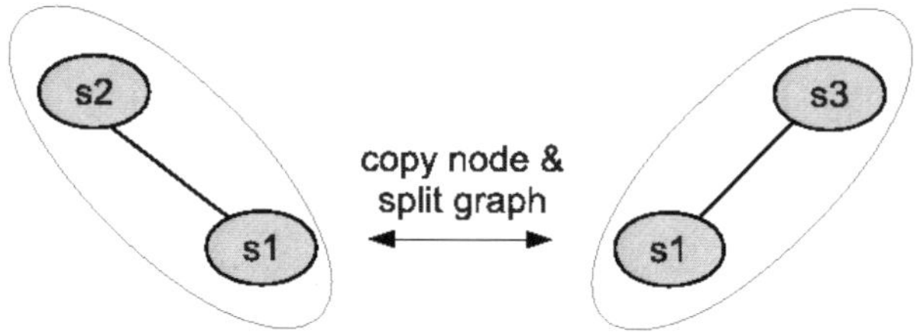

Figure 5: CONGA algorithm

highest split betweenness, if it is greater. The edge and node betweenness scores are then recalculated. In such a manner we can detect overlapping communities. Figure 5 shows the CONGA copying and splitting operations applied to our simple example, so that sentence s1 now exists in two communities.

The CONGO algorithm (Gregory, 2008) is an approximation of CONGA that is more efficient for large graphs. Girvan-Newman (and hence CONGA) are not feasible algorithms for very large graphs, due to the number of repeated betweenness calculations. CONGO addresses this problem by using *local betweenness* scores. Instead of calculating betweenness using the shortest paths of every pair of nodes in the graph, only nodes within a given horizon h of an edge are considered. When $h = \infty$ then CONGO and CONGA are identical. Gregory (Gregory, 2008) found good results using $h = 2$ or $h = 3$ on a variety of datasets including blog networks; here we experiment $h = 2$.

For the community detection step of our system, we run both CONGA and CONGO on our graphs and compare our results with the Girvan-Newman algorithm. For all community detection methods, as well as human annotations, any sentences that are not linked to at least one other sentence in Step 1 are assigned to their own singleton communities. Also, the algorithms we are evaluating are hierarchical (see Figure 4), and we evaluate at $n = 18$ clusters, since that is the average number of sentences per abstractive meeting summary in the training set.

5 Experimental Setup

In this section we describe the dataset used, including relevant annotations, as well as the statistical classifiers used for Step 1.

5.1 AMI Corpus

For these experiments we use the AMI meeting corpus (Carletta, 2006), specifically, the subset of scenario meetings where participants play roles within a fictional company. For each meeting, an annotator first authors an abstractive summary. Multiple annotators then create extractive summaries by linking sentences from the meeting transcript to sentences within the abstract. This generates a many-to-many mapping between transcript sentences and abstract sentences, so that a given transcript sentence can relate to more than one abstract sentence and vice-verse. A sample of this extractive-abstractive linking was shown in Figure 1.

It is known that inter-annotator agreement can be quite low for the summarization task (Mani et al., 1999; Mani, 2001b), and this is the case with the AMI extractive summarization codings. The average κ score is 0.45.

In these experiments, we use only human-authored transcripts and plan to use speech recognition transcripts in the future. Note that our overall approach is not specific to conversations or to speech data. Step 2 is completely general, while Step 1 uses a single *same-speaker* feature that is specific to conversations. That feature can be dropped to make our approach completely general (or, equivalently, that binary feature can be thought of as always 1 when applied to monologic text).

5.2 Classifiers

For Step 1, predicting abstractive links between sentences, we train a logistic regression classifier using the liblinear toolkit[2]. The training set consists of 98 meetings and there are nearly one million sentence pair instances since we consider every pairing of sentences within a meeting. The test set consists of 20 meetings on which we perform our evaluation.

6 Evaluation Metrics

In this section, we present our evaluation metrics for the two steps of the task.

6.1 Step 1 Evaluation: PRF and AUROC

For evaluating Step 1, predicting abstractive sentence links, we present both precision/recall/f-score

[2]http://www.csie.ntu.edu.tw/ cjlin/liblinear/

as well as the area under the receiver operator characteristic curve (AUROC). While the former scores evaluate the classifier at a particular posterior probability threshold, the AUROC evaluates the classifier more generally by comparing the true-positive and false-positive rates at varying probability thresholds.

6.2 Step 2 Evaluation: The Omega Index

For evaluating Step 2, ACD, we employ a metric called the Omega Index which is designed for comparing disjoint clustering solutions. To describe and motivate our use of this metric, it is necessary to describe previous metrics upon which the Omega Index improves. The Rand Index (Rand, 1971) is a way of comparing disjoint clustering solutions that is based on pairs of the objects being clustered. Two solutions are said to agree on a pair of objects if they each put both objects into the same cluster or each into different clusters. The Rand Index can then be formalized as

$$(a + d)/N$$

where N is the number of pairs of objects, a is the number of times the solutions agree on putting a pair in the same cluster and d is the number of times the solutions agree on putting a pair in different clusters. That is, the Rand Index is the number of pairs that are agreed on by the two solutions divided by the total number of pairs. The Rand Index is insufficient for overlapping solutions because pairs of objects can exist together in more than one community. In those cases, two solutions might agree on the occurrence of a pair of objects in one community but disagree on the occurrence of that pair in another community. The Rand Index cannot capture that distinction.

An improvement to the Rand Index is the Adjusted Rand Index (Hubert and Arabie, 1985) which adjusts the level of agreement according to the expected amount of agreement based on chance. However, the Adjusted Rand Index also cannot account for disjoint solutions.

The Omega Index (Collins and Dent, 1988) builds on both the Rand Index and Adjusted Rand Index by accounting for disjoint solutions and correcting for chance agreement. The Omega Index considers the *number* of clusters in which a pair of objects is together. The observed agreement between solutions is calculated by

$$Obs(s1, s2) = \sum_{j=0}^{min(J,K)} A_j/N$$

where J and K represent the maximum number of clusters in which any pair of objects appears together in solutions 1 and 2, respectively, A_j is the number of the pairs agreed by both solutions to be assigned to number of clusters j, and N is again the number of pairs of objects. That is, the observed agreement is the proportion of pairs classified the same way by the two solutions. The expected agreement is given by:

$$Exp(s1, s2) = \sum_{j=0}^{min(J,K)} N_{j_1} N_{j_2}/N^2$$

where N_{j_1} is the total number of pairs assigned to number of clusters j in solution 1, and N_{j_2} is the total number of pairs assigned to number of clusters j in solution 2. The Omega Index is then calculated as

$$Omega(s1, s2) = \frac{Obs(s1, s2) - Exp(s1, s2)}{1 - Exp(s1, s2)}$$

The numerator is the observed agreement adjusted by expected agreement, while the denominator is maximum possible agreement adjusted by expected agreement. The highest possible score of 1 indicates that two solutions perfectly agree on how each pair of objects is clustered. With the Omega Index, we can now evaluate the overlapping solutions discovered by our community detection algorithms.[3]

7 Results

In this section we present the results for both steps of ACD. Because the Omega Index is not used for evaluating Step 1, we keep that discussion brief.

7.1 Step 1 Results: Predicting Abstractive Sentence Links

For the task of predicting abstractive links within sentence pairs, the resulting graphs have an average of 133 nodes and 1730 edges, though this varies

[3]Software for calculating the Omega Index will be released upon publication of this paper.

System	Prec.	Rec.	F-Score	AUROC
Lower-Bound	0.18	1	0.30	0.50
Message Links	0.30	0.03	0.05	-
Abstractive Links	0.62	0.54	**0.54**	**0.89**

Table 1: P/R/F and AUROCs for Link Prediction

widely depending on meeting length (from 37 nodes and 61 edges for one short meeting to 224 edges and 5946 edges for a very long meeting). In comparison, the gold-standard graphs have an average of 113 nodes and 1360 edges. The gold-standards similarly show huge variation in graph size depending on meeting length.

Table 1 reports both the precision/recall/f-scores as well as the AUROC metrics. We compare our supervised classifier (labeled "Abstractive Links") with a lower-bound where all instances are predicted as positive, leading to perfect recall and low precision. Our system scores moderately well on both precision and recall, with an average f-score of 0.54. The AUROC for the abstractive link classifier is 0.89.

It is difficult to compare with previous work since, to our knowledge, nobody has previously modeled these extractive-abstractive mappings between document sentences and associated abstracts. We can compare with the results of Murray et al. (2010), however, who linked sentences by aggregating them into *messages*. In that work, each message is comprised of sentences that share a dialogue act type (e.g. an action item) and mention at least one common entity (e.g. *remote control*). Similar to our work, sentences can belong to more than one message. We assess how well their message-based approach captures these abstractive links, reporting their precision/recall/f-scores for this task in Table 1, with their system labeled "Message Links". While their precision is above the lower-bound, the recall and f-score are extremely low. This demonstrates that their notion of message links does not capture the phenomenon of abstractive sentence linking.

7.2 Step 2 Results: Discovering Abstractive Communities

For the task of discovering abstractive communities in our sentence graphs, Table 2 reports the Omega Index for the CONGA, CONGO and Girvan-Newman algorithms. We also report the average Omega Index for the human annotators themselves, derived by comparing each pair of annotator solutions for each meeting.

It is not surprising that the Omega Index is low for the inter-annotator comparison; we reported previously that the κ score for the extractive summaries of this corpus is 0.45. That κ score indicates that there is high disagreement about which sentences are most important in a meeting. We should not be surprised then that there is further disagreement about how the sentences are linked to one another. What *is* surprising is that the automatic community detection algorithms achieve higher Omega Index scores than do the annotators. Note that the higher scores of the community detection algorithms relative to human agreement is *not* simply an artefact of identifying clustering solutions that have more overlap than human solutions, since even the disjoint Girvan-Newman solutions are higher than inter-annotator levels. One possible explanation is that the annotators are engaged in a fairly local task when they create extractive summaries; for each abstractive sentence, they are looking for a set of sentences from the document that relate to that abstract sentence, and because of high redundancy in the document the different annotators choose subsets of sentences that have little overlap but are still similar (Supporting this, we have found that we can train on annotator A's extractive codings and test on annotator B's and get good classification results even if A and B have a low κ score.). In contrast, the community detection algorithms are taking a more comprehensive, global approach by considering all predicted links between sentences (Step 1) and identifying the overlapping communities among them (Step 2).

When looking for differences between automatic and human community detection, we observed that the algorithms assigned more overlap to sentences

System	Omega
Girvan-Newman	0.254
CONGA	**0.263**
CONGO	0.241
Human	0.209

Table 2: Omega Index for Community Detection

System	Omega All Annots.	Omega 1 Annot.
Girvan-Newman	0.445	0.878
CONGA	**0.454**	**0.896**
CONGO	0.453	0.894

Table 3: Omega Index, Gold-Standard Graphs

than did the human annotators. For example, the CONGA algorithm assigned each sentence to an average of 1.1 communities while the human annotators assigned each to an average of 1.04 communities. Note that every sentence belongs to at least one community since unlinked sentences belong to their own singleton communities, and most sentences are unlinked, explaining why both scores are close to 1.

Comparing the algorithms themselves, we find that CONGA is better than both Girvan-Newman (marginally significant, $p = 0.07$) and CONGO ($p = 0.015$) according to paired t-test. We believe that the superiority of CONGA over Girvan-Newman points to the importance of allowing overlapping communities. And while CONGO is an efficient approximation of CONGA that can be useful for very large graphs where CONGA and Girvan-Newman cannot be applied, in these experiments the local betweenness used by CONGO leads to lower overall scores. Furthermore, our networks are small enough that both CONGA and Girvan-Newman are able to finish quickly and there is therefore no need to rely on CONGO.

Our Step 2 results are dependent on the quality of the Step 1 results. We therefore test how good our community detection results would be if we had gold-standard graphs rather than the imperfect output from Step 1. We report two sets of results. In the first case, we take an annotator's gold-standard sentence graph showing links between sentences and proceed to run our algorithms over that graph, comparing our community detection results with the communities detected by all annotators. In the second case, we again take an annotator's gold-standard graph and apply our algorithms, but then only compare our community detection results with the communities detected by the annotator who supplied the gold-standard graph. Table 3 shows both sets of results. We can see that the latter set contains much higher scores, again reflecting that annotators disagree with each other on this task.

Given gold-standard sentence graphs, CONGA and CONGO perform very similarly; the differences are negligible. Both are substantially better than the Girvan-Newman algorithm (all $p < 0.01$). This tells us that it is necessary to employ community detection algorithms that allow overlapping communities. These results also tell us that the CONGO algorithm is more sensitive to errors in the Step 1 output since it performed well using the gold-standard but worse than Girvan-Newman when using the automatically derived graphs.

8 Conclusion

After giving an overview of the ACD task and our approach to it, we described how the Omega Index can be used as a summarization evaluation metric for this task, and explained why other community detection metrics are insufficient. The Omega Index is suitable because it can account for overlapping clustering solutions, and corrects for chance agreement.

The main surprising result was that all of the community detection algorithms have higher Omega Index scores than the human-human Omega scores representing annotator agreement. We have offered one possibe explanation; namely, that while the human annotators have numerous similar candidate sentences from the document that each could be linked to a given abstract sentence, they may be satisfied to only link (and thus extract) a small representative handful, whereas the community detection algorithms work to find all extractive-abstractive links. We plan to further research this issue, and potentially derive other evaluation metrics that better account for this phenomenon.

References

R. Barzilay and K. McKeown. 2005. Sentence fusion for multidocument news summarization. *Computational Linguistics*, 31(3):297–328.

J. Carbonell and J. Goldstein. 1998. The use of MMR, diversity-based reranking for reordering documents and producing summaries. In *Proc. of ACM SIGIR Conference on Research and Development in Information Retrieval 1998, Melbourne, Australia*, pages 335–336.

J. Carletta. 2006. Unleashing the killer corpus: experiences in creating the multi-everything ami meeting corpus. In *Proc. of LREC 2006, Genoa, Italy*, pages 181–190.

L. Collins and C. Dent. 1988. Omega: A general formulation of the rand index of cluster recovery suitable for non-disjoint solutions. *Multivariate Behavioral Research*, 23:231–242.

H. P. Edmundson. 1969. New methods in automatic extracting. *J. ACM*, 16(2):264–285.

M. Galley, K. McKeown, J. Hirschberg, and E. Shriberg. 2004. Identifying agreement and disagreement in conversational speech: Use of bayesian networks to model pragmatic dependencies. In *Proc. of ACL 2004*.

M. Girvan and M.E.J. Newman. 2002. Community structure in social and biological networks. *Proc. of the National Academy of Sciences*, 99:7821–7826.

S. Gregory. 2007. An algorithm to find overlapping community structure in networks. In *Proc. of ECML/PKDD 2007, Warsaw, Poland*.

S. Gregory. 2008. A fast algorithm to find overlapping communities in networks. In *Proc. of ECML/PKDD 2008, Antwerp, Belgium*.

L. Hubert and P. Arabie. 1985. Comparing partitions. *Journal of Classification*, 2:193–218.

S. Joty, G. Carenini, G. Murray, and R. Ng. 2010. Exploiting conversation structure in unsupervised topic segmentation for emails. In *Proc. of EMNLP 2010, Cambridge, MA, USA*.

D. Jurafsky and J. H. Martin, 2008. *Speech and Language Processing*. Prentice Hall.

H. P. Luhn. 1958. The automatic creation of literature abstracts. *IBM Journal of Research Development*, 2(2):159–165.

I. Malioutov and R. Barzilay. 2006. Minimum cut model for spoken lecture segmentation. In *Proc. of ACL 2006, Sydney, Australia*.

I. Mani, D. House, G. Klein, L. Hirschman, T. Firmin, and B. Sundheim. 1999. The TIPSTER SUMMAC text summarization evaluation. In *Proc. of EACL 1999, Bergen, Norway*, pages 77–85.

I. Mani. 2001a. *Automatic Summarization*. John Benjamin, Amsterdam, NL.

I. Mani. 2001b. Summarization evaluation: An overview. In *Proc. of the NTCIR Workshop 2 Meeting on Evaluation of Chinese and Japanese Text Retrieval and Text Summarization, Tokyo, Japan*, pages 77–85.

G. Murray, G. Carenini, and R. Ng. 2010. Generating and validating abstracts of meeting conversations: a user study. In *Proc. of INLG 2010, Dublin, Ireland*.

M. Porter, J-P. Onnela, and P. Mucha. 2009. Communities in networks. *Notices of the American Mathematical Society*, 56:1082–1097.

D. Radev, S. Blair-Goldensohn, and Z. Zhang. 2001. Experiments in single and multi-document summarization using MEAD. In *Proc. of DUC 2001, New Orleans, LA, USA*.

W.M. Rand. 1971. Objective criteria for the evaluation of clustering methods. *Journal of the American Statistical Association*, 66:846–850.

E. Shriberg, R. Dhillon, S. Bhagat, J. Ang, , and H. Carvey. 2004. The ICSI meeting recorder dialog act (MRDA) corpus. In *Proceedings of SIGdial Workshop on Discourse and Dialogue, Cambridge, MA, USA*, pages 97–100.

S. Teufel and M. Moens. 1997. Sentence extraction as a classification task. In *Proc. of ACL 1997, Workshop on Intelligent and Scalable Text Summarization, Madrid, Spain*, pages 58–65.

Machine Translation for Multilingual Summary Content Evaluation

Josef Steinberger and Marco Turchi
Joint Research Centre,
European Commission,
Via E. Fermi 2749,
21027 Ispra (VA), Italy
[name].[surname]@jrc.ec.europa.eu

Abstract

The multilingual summarization pilot task at TAC'11 opened a lot of problems we are facing when we try to evaluate summary quality in different languages. The additional language dimension greatly increases annotation costs. For the TAC pilot task English articles were first translated to other 6 languages, model summaries were written and submitted system summaries were evaluated. We start with the discussion whether ROUGE can produce system rankings similar to those received from manual summary scoring by measuring their correlation. We study then three ways of projecting summaries to a different language: projection through sentence alignment in the case of parallel corpora, simple summary translation and summarizing machine translated articles. Building such summaries gives opportunity to run additional experiments and reinforce the evaluation. Later, we investigate whether an evaluation based on machine translated models can perform close to an evaluation based on original models.

1 Introduction

Evaluation of automatically produced summaries in different languages is a challenging problem for the summarization community, because human efforts are multiplied to create model summaries for each language. Unavailability of parallel corpora suitable for news summarization adds even another annotation load because documents need to be translated to other languages. At the last TAC'11 campaign, six research groups spent a lot of work on creating evaluation resources in seven languages (Giannakopoulos et al., 2012). Thus compared to the monolingual evaluation, which requires writing model summaries and evaluating outputs of each system by hand, in the multilingual setting we need to obtain translations of all documents into the target language, write model summaries and evaluate the peer summaries for all the languages.

In the last fifteen years, research on Machine Translation (MT) has made great strides allowing human beings to understand documents written in various languages. Nowadays, on-line services such as *Google Translate* and *Bing Translator*[1] can translate text into more than 50 languages showing that MT is not a pipe-dream.

In this paper we investigate how machine translation can be plugged in to evaluate quality of summarization systems, which would reduce annotation efforts. We also discuss projecting summaries to different languages with the aim to reinforce the evaluation procedure (e.g. obtaining additional peers for comparison in different language or studying their language-independence).

This paper is structured as follows: after discussing the related work in section 2, we give a short overview of the TAC'11 multilingual pilot task (section 3). We compare average model and system manual scores and we also study ROUGE correlation to the manual scores. We run our experiments on a subset of languages of the TAC multilingual task corpus (English, French and Czech). Section 4 introduces our translation system. We mention its

[1] http://translate.google.com/ and http://www.microsofttranslator.com/

translation quality for language pairs used later in this study. Then we move on to the problem of projecting summaries to different languages in section 5. We discuss three approaches: projecting summary through sentence alignment in a parallel corpus, translating a summary, and summarizing translated source texts. Then, we try to answer the question whether using translated models produces similar system rankings as when using original models (section 6), accompanied by a discussion of discriminative power difference and cross-language model comparison.

2 Related work

Attempts of using machine translation in different natural language processing tasks have not been popular due to poor quality of translated texts, but recent advance in Machine Translation has motivated such attempts. In Information Retrieval, Savoy and Dolamic (2009) proposed a comparison between Web searches using monolingual and translated queries. On average, the results show a limited drop in performance, around 15% when translated queries are used.

In cross-language document summarization, Wan et al. (2010) and Boudin et al. (2010) combined the MT quality score with the informativeness score of each sentence to automatically produce summary in a target language. In Wan et al. (2010), each sentence of the source document is ranked according to both scores, the summary is extracted and then the selected sentences translated to the target language. Differently, in Boudin et al. (2010), sentences are first translated, then ranked and selected. Both approaches enhance the readability of the generated summaries without degrading their content.

Automatic evaluation of summaries has been widely investigated in the past. In the task of cross-lingual summarization evaluation Saggion et al. (2002) proposed different metrics to assess the content quality of a summary. Evaluation of summaries without the use of models has been introduced by Saggion et al. (2010). They showed that substituting models by full document in the computation of the Jensen-Shannon divergence measure can produce reliable rankings. Yeloglu et al. (2011) concluded that the pyramid method partially reflects the manual inspection of the summaries and ROUGE can only be used when there is a manually created summary. A method, and related resources, which allows saving precious annotation time and that makes the evaluation results across languages directly comparable was introduced by Turchi et al. (2010). This approach relies on parallel data and it is based on the manual selection of the most important sentences in a cluster of documents from a sentence-aligned parallel corpus, and by projecting the sentence selection to various target languages.

Our work addresses the same problem of reducing annotation time and generating models, but from a different prospective. Instead of using parallel data and annotation projection or full documents, we investigate the use of machine translation at different level of summary evaluation. While the aproach of Turchi et al. (2010) is focussed on sentence selection evaluation our strategy can also evaluate generative summaries, because it works on summary level.

3 TAC'11 Multilingual Pilot

The Multilingual task of TAC'11 (Giannakopoulos et al., 2012) aimed to evaluate the application of (partially or fully) language-independent summarization algorithms on a variety of languages. The task was to generate a representative summary (250 words) of a set of 10 related news articles.

The task included 7 languages (English, Czech, French, Hebrew, Hindi, Greek and Arabic). Annotation of each language sub-corpus was performed by a different group. English articles were manually translated to the target languages, 3 model summaries were written for each topic.

8 groups (systems) participated in the task, however, not all systems produced summaries for all languages. In addition there were 2 baselines: Centroid Baseline – the start of the centroid article and GA Topline – summary based on genetic algorithm using model summary information, which should serve as an upper bound.

Human annotators scored each summary, both models and peers, on the 5-to-1 scale (5 = the best, 1 = the worst) – human grades. The score corresponds to the overall responsiveness of the main TAC task – equal weight of content and readability. [2]

[2]In this article we focus on raw human grades. The task

	English	French	Czech	**average**	English	French	Czech	**average**
	Manual grades				Manual grades			
average model	4.06	4.03	4.73	**4.27**	4.06	4.03	4.73	**4.27**
average peer	2.73	2.18	2.56	**2.50**	2.73	2.18	2.56	**2.50**
	ROUGE-2				ROUGE-SU4			
average model	.194	.222	.206	**.207**	.235	.255	.237	**.242**
average peer	.139	.167	.182	**.163**	.183	.207	.211	**.200**
correlation to manual grading – peers and models not stemmed								
peers only	.574	.427	.444	**.482**	.487	.362	.519	**.456**
(p-value)	(< .1)							
models & peers	.735	.702	.484	**.640**	.729	.703	.549	**.660**
(p-value)	(< .01)	(< .02)			(< .02)	(< .02)		
correlation to manual grading – peers and models stemmed								
Peers only	.573	.445	.500	**.506**	.484	.336	.563	**.461**
(p-value)	(< .1)							
models & peers	.744	.711	.520	**.658**	.723	.700	.636	**.686**
(p-value)	(< .01)	(< .01)			(< .02)	(< .02)	(< .1)	

Table 1: Average ROUGE-2 and ROUGE-SU4 scores for models and peers, and their correlation to the manual evaluation (grades). We report levels of significance (p) for two-tailed test. Cells with missing p-values denote non-significant correlations ($p > .1$).

3.1 Manual Evaluation

When we look at the manually assigned grades we see that there is a clear gap between human and automatic summaries (see the first two rows in table 1). While the average grade for models were always over 4, peers were graded lower by 33% for English and by 54% for French and Czech. However, there were 5 systems for English and 1 system for French which were not significantly worse than at least one model.

3.2 ROUGE

The first question is: can an automatic metric rank the systems similarly as manual evaluation? This would be very useful when we test different configurations of our systems, in which case manual scoring is almost impossible. Another question is: can the metric distinguish well the gap between models and peers? ROUGE is widely used because of its simplicity and its high correlation with manually assigned content quality scores on overall system rankings, although per-case correlation is lower.

We investigated how the two most common ROUGE scores (ROUGE-2 and ROUGE-SU4) correlate with human grades. Although using n-grams with n greater than 1 gives limited possibility to reflect readability in the scores when compared to reference summaries, ROUGE is considered mainly as a content evaluation metric. Thus we cannot expect a perfect correlation because half of the grade assigned by humans reflects readability issues. ROUGE could not also evaluate properly the baselines. The centroid baseline contains a continuous text (the start of an article) and it thus gets higher grades by humans because of its good readability, but from the ROUGE point of view the baseline is weak. On the other hand, the topline used information from models and it is naturally more similar to them when evaluated by ROUGE. Its low readability ranked it lower in the case of human evaluation. Because of these problems we include in the correlation figures only the submitted systems, neither the baseline nor the topline.

Table 1 compares average model and peer ROUGE scores for the three analyzed languages. It adds two correlations[3] to human grades: for *models+systems* and for *systems only*. The first case should answer the question whether the automatic metric can distinguish between human and automatic summaries. The second settings could show

overview paper (Giannakopoulos et al., 2012) discusses, in addition, scaling down the grades of shorter summaries to avoid assigning better grades to shorter summaries.

[3]We used the classical Pearson correlation.

whether the automatic metric accurately evaluates the quality of automatic summaries. To ensure a fair comparison of models and non-models, each model summary is evaluated against two other models, and each non-model summary is evaluated three times, each time against a different couple of models, and these three scores are averaged out (the jackknifing procedure).[4] The difference of the model and system ROUGE scores is significant, although it is not that distinctive as in the case of human grades. The distinction results in higher correlations when we include models than in the more difficult *systems only* case. This is shown by both correlation figures and their confidence. The only significant correlation for the *systems only* case was for English and ROUGE-2. Other correlations did not cross the 90% confidence level. If we run ROUGE for morphologically rich languages (e.g. Czech), stemming plays more important role than in the case of English. In the case of French, which stands in between, we found positive effect of stemming only for ROUGE-2. ROUGE-2 vs. ROUGE-SU4: for English and French we see better correlation with ROUGE-2 but the free word ordering in Czech makes ROUGE-SU4 correlate better.

4 In-house Translator

Our translation service (Turchi et al., 2012) is based on the most popular class of Statistical Machine Translation systems (SMT): the Phrase-Based model (Koehn et al., 2003). It is an extension of the noisy channel model introduced by Brown et al. (1993), and uses phrases rather than words. A source sentence f is segmented into a sequence of I phrases $f^I = \{f_1, f_2, \ldots f_I\}$ and the same is done for the target sentence e, where the notion of phrase is not related to any grammatical assumption; a phrase is an n-gram. The best translation e_{best} of f is obtained by:

$$e_{best} = arg\max_e p(e|f) = arg\max_e p(f|e)p_{LM}(e)$$

$$= arg\max_e \prod_{i=1}^{I} \phi(f_i|e_i)^{\lambda_\phi} d(a_i - b_{i-1})^{\lambda_d} \prod_{i=1}^{|e|} p_{LM}(e_i|e_1 \ldots e_{i-1})^{\lambda_{LM}}$$

where $\phi(f_i|e_i)$ is the probability of translating a phrase e_i into a phrase f_i. $d(a_i - b_{i-1})$ is the distance-based reordering model that drives the system to penalize significant word reordering during translation, while allowing some flexibility. In the reordering model, a_i denotes the start position of the source phrase that is translated into the ith target phrase, and b_{i-1} denotes the end position of the source phrase translated into the $(i-1)$th target phrase. $p_{LM}(e_i|e_1 \ldots e_{i-1})$ is the language model probability that is based on the Markov's chain assumption. It assigns a higher probability to fluent/grammatical sentences. λ_ϕ, λ_{LM} and λ_d are used to give a different weight to each element. For more details see (Koehn et al., 2003). In this work we use the open-source toolkit Moses (Koehn et al., 2007).

Furthermore, our system takes advantage of a large in-house database of multi-lingual named and geographical entities. Each entity is identified in the source language and its translation is suggested to the SMT system. This solution avoids the wrong translation of those words which are part of a named entity and also common words in the source language, (e.g. "Bruno Le Maire" which can be wrongly translated to "Bruno Mayor"), and enlarges the source language coverage.

We built four models covering the following language pairs: En-Fr, En-Cz, Fr-En and Cz-En. To train them we use the freely available corpora: Europarl (Koehn, 2005), JRC-Acquis (Steinberger et al., 2006), CzEng0.9 (Bojar and Žabokrtský, 2009), Opus (Tiedemann, 2009), DGT-TM[5] and News Corpus (Callison-Burch et al., 2010), which results in more than 4 million sentence pairs for each model. Our system was tested on the News test set (Callison-Burch et al., 2010) released by the organizers of the 2010 Workshop on Statistical Machine Translation. Performance was evaluated using the Bleu score (Papineni et al., 2002): En-Fr 0.23, En-Cz 0.14, Fr-En 0.26 and Cz-En 0.22. The Czech

[4] In our experiments we used the same ROUGE settings as at TAC. The summaries were truncated to 250 words. For English we used the Porter stemmer included in the ROUGE package, for Czech the aggressive version from `http://members.unine.ch/jacques.savoy/clef/index.html` and for French `http://jcs.mobile-utopia.com/jcs/19941\_FrenchStemmer.java`.

[5] `http://langtech.jrc.it/DGT-TM.html`

language is clearly more challenging than French for the SMT system, this is due to the rich morphology and the partial free word order. These aspects are more evident when we translate to Czech, for which we have poor results.

5 Mapping Peers to Other Languages

When we want to generate a summary of a set of articles in a different language we have different possibilities. The first case is when we have articles in the target language and we run our summarizer on them. This was done in the Multilingual TAC task. If we have parallel corpora we can take advantage of projecting a sentence-extractive summary from one language to another (see Section 5.1).

If we do not have the target language articles we can apply machine translation to get them and run the summarizer on them (see Section 5.3). If we miss a crucial resource for running the summarizer for the target language we can simply translate the summaries (see Section 5.2).

In the case of the TAC Multilingual scenario these projections can also give us summaries for all languages from the systems which were applied only on some languages.

5.1 Aligned Summaries

Having a sentence-aligned (parallel) corpus gives access to additional experiments. Because the current trend is still on the side of pure sentence extraction we can investigate whether the systems select the same sentences across the languages. While creating the TAC corpus each research group translated the English articles into their language, thus the resulting corpus was close to be parallel. However, sentences are not always aligned one-to-one because a translator may decide, for stylistic or other reasons, to split a sentence into two or to combine two sentences into one. Translations and original texts are never perfect, so that it is also possible that the translator accidentally omits or adds some information, or even a whole sentence. For these reasons, aligners such as Vanilla[6], which implements the Gale and Church algorithm (Gale and Church, 1994), typically also allow two-to-one, one-to-two, zero-to-one and one-to-zero sentence alignments. Alignments other than one-to-one thus present a challenge for the method of aligning two text, in particular one-to-two and two-to-one alignments. We used Vanilla to align Czech and English article sentences, but because of high error rate we corrected the alignment by hand.

The English summaries were then aligned to Czech (and the opposite direction as well) according to the following approach. Sentences in a source language system summary were split. For each sentence we found the most similar sentence in the source language articles based on 3-gram overlap. The alignment information was used to select sentences for the target language summary. Some simplification rules were applied: if the most similar sentence found in the source articles was aligned with more sentences in the target language articles, all the projected sentences were selected (one-to-two alignment); if the sentence to be projected covered only a part of sentences aligned with one target language sentence, the target language sentence was selected (two-to-one alignment).

The 4th row in table 2 shows average peer ROUGE scores of aligned summaries.[7] When comparing the scores to the peers in original language (3rd row) we notice that the average peer score is slightly better in the case of English (cz→en projection) and significantly worse for Czech (en→cz projection) indicating that Czech summaries were more similar to English models than English summaries to Czech models.

Having the alignment we can study the overlap of the same sentences selected by a summarizer in different languages. The peer average for the en-cz language pair was 31%, meaning that only a bit less than one third of sentences was selected both to English and Czech summaries by the same system. The percentage differed a lot from a summarizer to another one, from 13% to 57%. This number can be seen as an indicator of summarizer's language independence.

However, the system rankings of aligned summaries did not correlate well with human grades. There are many inaccuracies in the alignment summary creation process. At first, finding the sentence

[6]http://nl.ijs.si/telri/Vanilla/

[7]Models are usually not sentence-extractive and thus aligning them would not make much sense.

	ROUGE-2					ROUGE-SU4				
	fr→en	cz→en	en→fr	en→cz	**avg.**	fr→en	cz→en	en→fr	en→cz	**avg.**
	average ROUGE scores									
orig. model	.194	.194	.222	.206	**.207**	.235	.235	.255	.237	**.242**
transl. model	.128	.162	.187	.123	**.150**	.184	.217	.190	.160	**.188**
orig. peer	.139	.139	.167	.182	**.163**	.183	.183	.207	.211	**.200**
aligned peer		.148		.146	**.147**		.175		.140	**.180**
transl. peer	.100	.119	.128	.102	**.112**	.155	.174	.179	.140	**.162**
	correlation to source language manual grading for translated summaries									
peers only	.411	.483	.746	.456	**.524**	.233	.577	.754	.571	**.534**
(p-value)			(< .05)					(< .05)		
models & peers	.622	.717	.835	.586	**.690**	.581	.777	.839	.620	**.704**
(p-value)	(< .05)	(< .05)	(< .01)	(< .1)		(< .05)	(< .02)	(< .01)	(< .05)	
	correlation to target language manual grading for translated summaries									
peers only	.685	.708	.555	.163	**.528**	.516	.754	.529	.267	**.517**
(p-value)	(< .1)									

Table 2: ROUGE results of translated summaries, evaluated against target language models (e.g., cz→en against English models).

in the source data that was probably extracted is strongly dependent on the sentence splitting each summarizer used. At second, alignment relations different from one-to-one results in selecting content with different length compared to the original summary. And since ROUGE measures recall, and truncates the summaries, it introduces another inaccuracy. There were also relations one-to-zero (sentences not translated to the target language). In that case no content was added to the target summary.

5.2 Translated Summaries

The simplest way to obtain a summary in a different language is to apply machine translation software on summaries. Here we investigate (table 2) whether machine translation errors affect the system order by correlation to human grades again. In this case we have two reference human grade sets: one for the source language (from which we translate) and one for the target language (to which we translate). Since there were different models for each language we can include models only in computing the correlation against source language manual grading.

At first, we can see that ROUGE scores are affected by the translation errors. Average model ROUGE-2 score went down by 28% and average peer ROUGE-2 by 31%. ROUGE-SU4 seems to be more robust to deal with the translation errors: models went down by 21%, peers by 19%. The gap between models and peers is still distinguishable, system ranking correlation to human grades holds similar levels although less statistically significant correlations can be seen. Clearly, quality of the translator affects these results because our worst translator (en→cz) produced the worst summaries. Correlation to the source language manual grades indicates how the ranking of the summarizers is affected (changed) by translation errors. For example it compares ranking for English based on manual grades with ranking computed on the same summaries translated from English to French. The second scenario (correlation to target language scores) shows how similar is the ranking of summarizers based on translated summaries with the target language ranking based on original summaries. If we omit translation inaccuracies, low correlation in the latter case indicates qualitatively different output of participating peers (e.g. en and cz summaries).

5.3 Summarizing Translated Articles

To complete the figure we tested the configuration in which we first translate the full articles to the target language and then apply a summarizer. As we have at disposal an implementation of system 3 from the TAC multilingual task we used it on 4 translated document sets (en→cz, cz→en, fr→en, en→fr). This system was the best according to human grades in all three discussed languages.

method	ROUGE-2	ROUGE-SU4
en	.177	.209
cz → en alignment	.200	.235
cz → en translation	.142	.194
en from (cz → en source translation)	**.132**	**.181**
fr → en translation	.120	.172
en from (fr → en source translation)	**.129**	**.185**
fr	.214	.241
en → fr translation	.167	.212
fr from (en → fr source translation)	**.156**	**.202**
cz	.204	.225
en → cz alignment	.176	.196
en → cz translation	.115	.150
cz from (en → cz source translation)	**.138**	**.178**

Table 3: ROUGE results of different variants of summaries produced by system 3. The first line shows the ROUGE scores of the original English summaries submitted by system 3. The second line gives average scores of the cz→en aligned summaries (see Section 5.1), in the 3rd and 5th lines there are figures of cz→en and fr→en translated summaries, and 4th and 6th lines show scores when the summarizer was applied on translated source texts (cz→en and fr→en). Similarly, lines further down show performance for French and Czech.

The system is based on the latent semantic analysis framework originally proposed by Gong and Liu (2002) and later improved by J. Steinberger and Ježek (2004). It first builds a term-by-sentence matrix from the source articles, then applies Singular Value Decomposition (SVD) and finally uses the resulting matrices to identify and extract the most salient sentences. SVD finds the latent (orthogonal) dimensions, which in simple terms correspond to the different topics discussed in the source (for details see (Steinberger et al., 2011)).

Table 3 shows all results of summaries generated by the summarizer. The first part compares English summaries. We see that when projecting the summary through alignment from Czech, see Section 5.1, a better summary was obtained. When using translation the summaries are always significantly worse compared to original (TAC) summaries, with the lowest performing en→cz translation. It is interesting that in the case of this low-performing translator it was significantly better to translate the source articles and to use the summarizer afterwards. The advantage of this configuration is that the core of the summarizer (LSA) treats all terms the same way, thus even English terms that were not translated work well for sentence selection. On the other hand, when translating the summary ROUGE will not match the English terms in Czech models.

6 Using Translated Models

With growing number of languages the annotation effort rises (manual creation of model summaries). Now we investigate whether we can produce models in one pivot language (e.g., English) and translate them automatically to all other languages. The fact that in the TAC corpus we have manual summaries for each language gives us opportunity to reinforce the evaluation by translating all model summaries to a common language and thus obtaining a larger number of models. This way we can also evaluate similarity among models coming from different languages and it lowers the annotators' subjectivity.

6.1 Evaluation Against Translated Models

Table 4 shows ROUGE figures when peers were evaluated against translated models. We discuss also the case when English peer summaries (and models as well) are evaluated against both French and Czech models translated to English. We can see again lower ROUGE scores caused by translation errors, however, there is more or less the same gap between peers and models and the correlation holds similar levels as when using the original target language models. Exceptions are using English models translated to French and Czech models translated to English in combination with the *systems only* correlation. If we used both French and Czech mod-

	ROUGE-2						ROUGE-SU4					
peers from	en			fr	cz	**avg.**	en			fr	cz	**avg.**
models tr. from	fr	cz	fr / cz	en	en		fr	cz	fr / cz	en	en	
average model	.144	.167	.155	.165	.144	**.155**	.207	.221	.206	.215	.190	**.208**
average peer	.110	.111	.104	.135	.125	**.117**	.170	.162	.153	.186	.172	**.169**
	correlation to target language manual grading											
peers only	.639	.238	.424	.267	.541	**.422**	.525	.136	.339	.100	.624	**.345**
(p-value)	< .1											
models & peers	.818	.717	.782	.614	.520	**.690**	.785	.692	.759	.559	.651	**.793**
(p-value)	< .01	< .02	< .01	< .05			< .01	< .02	< .01	< .1	< .1	

Table 4: ROUGE results of using translated model summaries, which evaluate both peer and model summaries in the particular language.

els translated to English, higher correlation of English peers with translated French models was averaged out by lower correlation with Czech models. And because the TAC Multilingual task contained 7 languages the experiment can be extended to using translated models from 6 languages. However, our results rather indicate that using the best translator is better choice.

Given the small scale of the experiment we cannot draw strong conclusions on discriminative power[8] when using translated models. However, our experiments indicate that by using translated summaries we are partly loosing discriminative power (i.e. ROUGE finds fewer significant differences between systems).

6.2 Comparing Models Across Languages

By translating both Czech and French models to English we could compare all models against each other. For each topic we had 9 models: 3 original English models, 3 translated from French and 3 from Czech. In this case we reached slightly better correlations for the *models+systems* case: ROUGE-2: .790, ROUGE-SU4: .762. It was mainly because of the fact that this time also *models only* rankings from ROUGE correlated with human grades (ROUGE-2: .475, ROUGE-SU4: .445). When we used only English models, the models ranking did not correlate at all (≈ -0.1). Basically, one English model was less similar to the other two, but it did not mean that it was worse which was shown by adding models from other languages. If we do not have enough reference summaries this could be a way to lower subjectivity in the evaluation process.

[8] Discriminative power measures how successful the automatic measure is in finding the same significant differences between systems as manual evaluation.

7 Conclusion

In this paper we discuss the synergy between machine translation and multilingual summarization evaluation. We show how MT can be used to obtain both peer and model evaluation data.

Summarization evaluation mostly aims to achieve two main goals a) to identify the absolute performance of each system and b) to rank all the systems according to their performances. Our results show that the use of translated summaries or models does not alter much the overall system ranking. It maintains a fair correlation with the source language ranking although without statistical significance in most of the *systems only* cases given the limited data set. A drop in ROUGE score is evident, and it strongly depends on the translation performance. The use of aligned summaries, which limits the drop, requires high quality parallel data and alignments, which are not always available and have a significant cost to be created.

The study leaves many opened questions: What is the required translation quality which would let us substitute target language models? Are translation errors averaged out when using translated models from more languages? Can we add a new language to the TAC multilingual corpus just by using MT having in mind lower quality (→ lower scores) and being able to quantify the drop? Experimenting with a larger evaluation set could try to find the answers.

References

O. Bojar and Z. Žabokrtský. 2009. CzEng0.9: Large Parallel Treebank with Rich Annotation. *Prague Bulletin of Mathematical Linguistics*, 92. in print.

F. Boudin, S. Huet, J.M. Torres-Moreno, and J.M. Torres-Moreno. 2010. A graph-based approach to cross-language multi-document summarization. *Research journal on Computer science and computer engineering with applications (Polibits)*, 43:113–118.

P.F. Brown, V.J.D. Pietra, S.A.D. Pietra, and R.L. Mercer. 1993. The mathematics of statistical machine translation: Parameter estimation. *Computational linguistics*, 19(2):263–311.

C. Callison-Burch, P. Koehn, C. Monz, K. Peterson, M. Przybocki, and O.F. Zaidan. 2010. Findings of the 2010 joint workshop on statistical machine translation and metrics for machine translation. In *Proceedings of the Joint Fifth Workshop on Statistical Machine Translation and MetricsMATR*, pages 17–53. Association for Computational Linguistics.

W.A. Gale and K.W. Church. 1994. A program for aligning sentences in bilingual corpora. *Computational linguistics*, 19.

G. Giannakopoulos, M. El-Haj, B. Favre, M. Litvak, J. Steinberger, and V. Varma. 2012. Tac 2011 multiling pilot overview. In *Proceedings of TAC'11*. NIST.

Y. Gong and X. Liu. 2002. Generic text summarization using relevance measure and latent semantic analysis. In *Proceedings of ACM SIGIR*, New Orleans, US.

P. Koehn, F.J. Och, and D. Marcu. 2003. Statistical phrase-based translation. In *Proceedings of the 2003 Conference of the North American Chapter of the Association for Computational Linguistics on Human Language Technology-Volume 1*, pages 48–54. Association for Computational Linguistics.

P. Koehn, H. Hoang, A. Birch, C. Callison-Burch, M. Federico, N. Bertoldi, B. Cowan, W. Shen, C. Moran, R. Zens, et al. 2007. Moses: Open source toolkit for statistical machine translation. In *Proceedings of the 45th Annual Meeting of the ACL on Interactive Poster and Demonstration Sessions*, pages 177–180. Association for Computational Linguistics.

P. Koehn. 2005. Europarl: A parallel corpus for statistical machine translation. In *Proceedings of the MT summit*, volume 5.

K. Papineni, S. Roukos, T. Ward, and W.J. Zhu. 2002. Bleu: a method for automatic evaluation of machine translation. In *Proceedings of the 40th annual meeting on association for computational linguistics*, pages 311–318. Association for Computational Linguistics.

H. Saggion, D. Radev, S. Teufel, W. Lam, and S.M. Strassel. 2002. Developing infrastructure for the evaluation of single and multi-document summarization systems in a cross-lingual environment. In *Proceedings of LREC 2002*, pages 747–754.

H. Saggion, J.M. Torres-Moreno, I. Cunha, and E. SanJuan. 2010. Multilingual summarization evaluation without human models. In *Proceedings of the 23rd International Conference on Computational Linguistics: Posters*, pages 1059–1067. Association for Computational Linguistics.

J. Savoy and L. Dolamic. 2009. How effective is google's translation service in search? *Communications of the ACM*, 52(10):139–143.

J. Steinberger and K. Ježek. 2004. Text summarization and singular value decomposition. In *Proceedings of the 3rd ADVIS conference*, Izmir, Turkey.

R. Steinberger, B. Pouliquen, A. Widiger, C. Ignat, T. Erjavec, D. Tufis, and D. Varga. 2006. The jrc-acquis: A multilingual aligned parallel corpus with 20+ languages. *Arxiv preprint cs/0609058*.

J. Steinberger, M. Kabadjov, R. Steinberger, H. Tanev, M. Turchi, and V. Zavarella. 2011. Jrcs participation at tac 2011: Guided and multilingual summarization tasks. In *Proceedings of the Text Analysis Conference (TAC)*.

J. Tiedemann. 2009. News from opus-a collection of multilingual parallel corpora with tools and interfaces. In *Proceedings of the Recent Advances in Natural Language Processing Conference*, volume 5, pages 237–248. John Benjamins Amsterdam.

M. Turchi, J. Steinberger, M. Kabadjov, and R. Steinberger. 2010. Using parallel corpora for multilingual (multi-document) summarisation evaluation. In *Proceedings of the Multilingual and Multimodal Information Access Evaluation Conference*, pages 52–63. Springer.

M. Turchi, M. Atkinson, A. Wilcox, B. Crawley, S. Bucci, R. Steinberger, and E. Van der Goot. 2012. Onts:optima news translation system. In *Proceedings of EACL 2012*, page 25.

X. Wan, H. Li, and J. Xiao. 2010. Cross-language document summarization based on machine translation quality prediction. In *Proceedings of the 48th Annual Meeting of the Association for Computational Linguistics*, pages 917–926. Association for Computational Linguistics.

O. Yeloglu, E. Milios, and N. Zincir-Heywood. 2011. Multi-document summarization of scientific corpora. In *Proceedings of the 2011 ACM Symposium on Applied Computing*, pages 252–258. ACM.

Ecological Validity and the Evaluation of Speech Summarization Quality

Anthony McCallum
University of Toronto
40 St. George Street
Toronto, ON, Canada
mccallum@cs.toronto.edu

Cosmin Munteanu
National Research Council Canada
46 Dineen Drive
Fredericton, NB, Canada
cosmin.munteanu@nrc-cnrc.gc.ca

Gerald Penn
University of Toronto
40 St. George Street
Toronto, ON, Canada
gpenn@cs.toronto.edu

Xiaodan Zhu
National Research Council Canada
1200 Montreal Road
Ottawa, ON, Canada
xiaodan.zhu@nrc-cnrc.gc.ca

Abstract

There is little evidence of widespread adoption of speech summarization systems. This may be due in part to the fact that the natural language heuristics used to generate summaries are often optimized with respect to a class of evaluation measures that, while computationally and experimentally inexpensive, rely on subjectively selected gold standards against which automatically generated summaries are scored. This evaluation protocol does not take into account the usefulness of a summary in assisting the listener in achieving his or her goal.

In this paper we study how current measures and methods for evaluating summarization systems compare to human-centric evaluation criteria. For this, we have designed and conducted an ecologically valid evaluation that determines the value of a summary when embedded in a task, rather than how closely a summary resembles a gold standard. The results of our evaluation demonstrate that in the domain of lecture summarization, the well-known baseline of maximal marginal relevance (Carbonell and Goldstein, 1998) is statistically significantly worse than human-generated extractive summaries, and even worse than having no summary at all in a simple quiz-taking task. Priming seems to have no statistically significant effect on the usefulness of the human summaries. In addition, ROUGE scores and, in particular, the context-free annotations that are often supplied to ROUGE as references, may not always be reliable as inexpensive proxies for ecologically valid evaluations. In fact, under some conditions, relying exclusively on ROUGE may even lead to scoring human-generated summaries that are inconsistent in their usefulness relative to using no summaries very favourably.

1 Background and Motivation

Summarization maintains a representation of an entire spoken document, focusing on those utterances (sentence-like units) that are most important and therefore does not require the user to process everything that has been said. Our work focuses on extractive summarization where a selection of utterances is chosen from the original spoken document in order to make up a summary.

Current speech summarization research has made extensive use of intrinsic evaluation measures such as F-measure, Relative Utility, and ROUGE (Lin, 2004), which score summaries against subjectively selected gold standard summaries obtained using human annotators. These annotators are asked to arbitrarily select (in or out) or rank utterances, and in doing so commit to relative salience judgements with no attention to goal orientation and no requirement to synthesize the meanings of larger units of structure into a coherent message.

Given this subjectivity, current intrinsic evaluation measures are unable to properly judge which summaries are useful for real-world applications. For example, intrinsic evaluations have failed to show that summaries created by algorithms based on complex linguistic and acoustic features are better than baseline summaries created by simply choosing the positionally first utterances or longest utterances in a spoken document (Penn and Zhu, 2008). What is needed is an ecologically valid evaluation that determines how valuable a summary is when embedded in a task, rather than how closely a summary matches the subjective utterance level scores assigned by annotators.

Ecological validity is "the ability of experiments to tell us how real people operate in the real world" (Cohen, 1995). This is often obtained by using human judges, but it is important to realize that the mere use of human subjects provides no guarantee as to the ecological validity of their judgements. When utterances are merely ranked with numerical scores out of context, for example, the human judges who perform this task are not performing a task that they generally perform in their daily lives, nor does the task correspond to how they would create or use a good summary if they did have a need for one. In fact, there may not even be a guarantee that they *understand* the task --- the notions of "importance," "salience" and the like, when defining the criterion by which utterances are selected, are not easy to circumscribe. Judgements obtained in this fashion are no better than those of the generative linguists who leaned back in their armchairs in the 1980s to introspect on the grammaticality of natural language sentences. The field of computational linguistics could only advance when corpora became electronically available to investigate language that was written in an ecologically valid context.

Ours is not the first ecologically valid experiment to be run in the context of speech summarization, however. He et al. (1999; 2000) conducted a very thorough and illuminating study of speech summarization in the lecture domain that showed (1) speech summaries are indeed very useful to have around, if they are done properly, and (2) abstractive summaries do not seem to add any statistically significant advantage to the quality of a summary over what topline extractive summaries can provide. This is very good news; extractive summaries are worth creating. Our study extends this work by attempting to evaluate the relative quality of extractive summaries. We conjecture that it would be very difficult for this field to progress unless we have a means of accurately measuring extractive summarization quality. Even if the measure comes at great expense, it is important to do.

Another noteworthy paper is that of Liu and Liu (2010), who, in addition to collecting human summaries of six meetings, conducted a subjective assessment of the quality of those summaries with numerically scored questionnaires. These are known as *Likert scales*, and they form an important component of any human-subject study in the field of human-computer interaction. Liu and Liu (2010) cast considerable doubt on the value of ROUGE relative to these questionnaires. We will focus here on an objective, task-based measure that typically complements those subjective assessments.

2 Spontaneous Speech

Spontaneous speech is often not linguistically well-formed, and contains disfluencies, such as false starts, filled pauses, and repetitions. Additionally, spontaneous speech is more vulnerable to automatic speech recognition (ASR) errors, resulting in a higher word error rate (WER). As such, speech summarization has the most potential for domains consisting of spontaneous speech (e.g. lectures, meeting recordings). Unfortunately, these domains are not easy to evaluate compared to highly structured domains such as broadcast news. Furthermore, in broadcast news, nearly perfect studio acoustic conditions and professionally trained readers results in low ASR WER, making it an easy domain to summarize. The result is that most research has been conducted in this domain. However, a positional baseline performs very well in summarizing broadcast news (Christensen, 2004), meaning that simply taking the first N utterances provides a very challenging baseline, questioning the value of summarizing this domain. In addition, the widespread availability of written sources on the same topics means that there is not a strong use case for speech summarization over simply summarizing the equivalent textual articles on which the news broadcasts were based. This makes it even more difficult to preserve ecological validity.

University lectures present a much more relevant domain, with less than ideal acoustic conditions but structured presentations in which deviation from written sources (e.g., textbooks) is commonplace. Here, a positional baseline performs very poorly. The lecture domain also lends itself well to a task-based evaluation measure; namely university level quizzes or exams. This constitutes a real-world problem in a domain that is also representative of other spontaneous speech domains that can benefit from speech summarization.

3 Ecologically Valid Evaluation

As pointed out by Penn and Zhu (2008), current speech summarizers have been optimized to perform an utterance selection task that may not necessarily reflect how a summarizer is able to capture the goal orientation or purpose of the speech data. In our study, we follow methodologies established in the field of Human-Computer Interaction (HCI) for evaluating an algorithm or system – that is, determining the benefits a system brings to its users, namely usefulness, usability, or utility, in allowing a user to reach a specific goal. Increasingly, such user-centric evaluations are carried out within various natural language processing applications (Munteanu et al., 2006). The prevailing trend in HCI is for conducting extrinsic summary evaluations (He et al., 2000; Murray et al., 2008; Tucker et al., 2010), where the value of a summary is determined by how well the summary can be used to perform a specific task rather than comparing the content of a summary to an artificially created gold standard. We have conducted an ecologically valid evaluation of speech summarization that has evaluated summaries under real-world conditions, in a task-based manner.

The university lecture domain is an example of a domain where summaries are an especially suitable tool for navigation. Simply performing a search will not result in the type of understanding required of students in their lectures. Lectures have topics, and there is a clear communicative goal. For these reasons, we have chosen this domain for our evaluation. By using actual university lectures as well as university students representative of the users who would make use of a speech summarization system in this domain, all results obtained are ecologically valid.

3.1 Experimental Overview

We conducted a within-subject experiment where participants were provided with first year sociology university lectures on a lecture browser system installed on a desktop computer. For each lecture, the browser made accessible the audio, manual transcripts, and an optional summary. Evaluation of a summary was based on how well the user of the summary was able to complete a quiz based on the content of the original lecture material.

It is important to note that not all extrinsic evaluation is ecologically valid. To ensure ecological validity in this study, great care was taken to ensure that human subjects were placed under conditions that result in behavior that would be expected in actual real-world tasks.

3.2 Evaluation

Each quiz consisted of 12 questions, and were designed to be representative of what students were expected to learn in the class, incorporating factual questions only, to ensure that variation in participant intelligence had a minimal impact on results. In addition, questions involved information that was distributed equally throughout the lecture, but at the same time not linearly in the transcript or audio slider, which would have allowed participants to predict where the next answer might be located. Finally, questions were designed to avoid content that was thought to be common knowledge in order to minimize the chance of participants having previous knowledge of the answers.

All questions were short answer or fill-in-the-blank. Each quiz consisted of an equal number of four distinct types of questions, designed so that performing a simple search would not be effective, though no search functionality was provided. Question types do not appear in any particular order on the quiz and were not grouped together.

Type 1: These questions can be answered simply by looking at the slides. As such, these questions could be answered correctly with or without a summary as slides were available in all conditions.

Type 2: Slides provide an indication of where the content required to answer these questions are located. Access to the corresponding utterances is still required to find the answer to the questions.

Type 3: Answers to these questions can only be found in the transcript and audio. The slides provide no hint as to where the relevant content is located.

Type 4: These questions are more complicated and require a certain level of topic comprehension. These questions often require connecting concepts from various portions of the lecture. These questions are more difficult and were included to minimize the chance that participants would already know the answer to questions without watching the lecture.

A teaching assistant for the sociology class from which our lectures were obtained generated the quizzes used in the evaluation. This teaching assistant had significant experience in the course, but was not involved in the design of this study and did not have any knowledge relating to our hypotheses or the topic of extractive summarization. These quizzes provided an ecologically valid quantitative measure of whether a given summary was useful. Having this evaluation metric in place, automated summaries were compared to manual summaries created by each participant in a previous session.

3.3 Participants

Subjects were recruited from a large university campus, and were limited to undergraduate students who had at least two terms of university studies, to ensure familiarity with the format of university-level lectures and quizzes. Students who had taken the first year sociology course we drew lectures from were not permitted to participate. The study was conducted with 48 participants over the course of approximately one academic semester.

3.4 Method

Each evaluation session began by having a participant perform a short warm-up with a portion of lecture content, allowing the participant to become familiar with the lecture browser interface. Following this, the participant completed four quizzes, one for each of four lecture-condition combinations. There were a total of four lectures and four conditions. Twelve minutes were given for each quiz. During this time, the participant was able to browse the audio, slides, and summary. Each lecture was about forty minutes in length, establishing a time constraint. Lectures and conditions were rotated using a Latin square for counter balancing. All participants completed each of the four conditions.

One week prior to his or her evaluation session, each participant was brought in and asked to listen to and summarize the lectures beforehand. This resulted in the evaluation simulating a scenario where someone has heard a lecture at least one week in the past and may or may not remember the content during an exam or quiz. This is similar to conditions most university students experience.

3.5 Conditions

The lecture audio recordings were manually transcribed and segmented into utterances, determined by 200 millisecond pauses, resulting in segments that correspond to natural sentences or phrases. The task of summarization consisted of choosing a set of utterances for inclusion in a summary (extractive summarization), where the total summary length was bounded by 17-23% of the words in the lecture; a percentage typical to most summarization scoring tasks. All participants were asked to make use of the browser interface for four lectures, one for each of the following conditions: *no summary*, *generic manual summary*, *primed manual summary*, and *automatic summary*.

No summary: This condition served as a baseline where no summary was provided, but participants had access to the audio and transcript. While all lecture material was provided, the twelve-minute time constraint made it impossible to listen to the lecture in its entirety.

Generic manual summary: I this condition, each participant was provided with a manually generated summary. Each summary was created by the participant him or herself in a previous session. Only audio and text from the in-summary utterances were available for use. This condition demonstrates how a manually created summary is able to aid in the task of taking a quiz on the subject matter.

Primed manual summary: Similar to above, in this condition, a summary was created manually by selecting a set of utterances from the lecture transcript. For primed summaries, full access to a priming quiz, containing all of the questions in the evaluation quiz as well as several additional questions, was available at the time of summary creation. This determines the value of creating summaries with a particular task in mind, as opposed to simply choosing utterances that are felt to be most important or salient.

Automatic summary: The procedure for this condition was identical to the *generic manual summary* condition from the point of view of the participant. However, during the evaluation phase, an automatically generated summary was provided instead of the summary that the participant created him or herself. The algorithm used to generate this summary was an implementation of MMR (Carbonell and Goldstein, 1998). Cosine similarity with tf-idf term weighting was used to calculate similarity. Although the redundancy component of MMR makes it especially suitable for multi-document summarization, there is no negative effect if redundancy is not an issue. It is worth noting that our lectures are longer than material typically summarized, and lectures in general are more likely to contain redundant material than a domain such as broadcast news. There was only one MMR summary generated for each lecture, meaning that multiple participants made use of identical summaries. The automatic summary was created by adding the highest scoring utterances one at a time until the sum of the length of all of the selected utterances reached 20% of the number of words in the original lecture. MMR was chosen as it is commonly used in summarization. MMR is a competitive baseline, even among state-of-art summarization algorithms, which tend to correlate well with it.

What this protocol does not do is pit several strategies for automatic summary generation against each other. That study, where more advanced summarization algorithms will also be examined, is forthcoming. The present experiments have the collateral benefit of serving as a means for collecting ecologically valid human references for that study.

3.6 Results

Quizzes were scored by a teaching assistant for the sociology course from which the lectures were taken. Quizzes were marked as they would be in the actual course and each question was graded with equal weight out of two marks. The scores were then converted to a percentage. The resulting scores (Table 1) are 49.3+-17.3% for the *no summary* condition, 48.0+-16.2% for the *generic manual summary* condition, 49.1+-15.2% for the *primed summary* condition, and 41.0+-16.9% for *MMR*. These scores are lower than averages expected in a typical university course. This can be partially attributed to the existence of a time constraint.

Condition	Average Quiz Score
no summary	49.3+-17.3%
generic manual summary	48.0+-16.2%
primed manual summary	49.1+-15.2%
automatic summary (MMR)	41.0+-16.9%

Table 1. Average Quiz Scores

Execution of the Shapiro-Wilk Test confirmed the scores are normally distributed and Mauchly's Test of Sphericity indicates that the sphericity assumption holds. Skewness and Kurtosis tests were also employed to confirm normality. A repeated measures ANOVA determined that scores varied significantly between conditions ($F(3,141)=5.947$, $P=0.001$). Post-hoc tests using the Bonferroni correction indicate that the *no summary*, *generic manual summary*, and *primed manual summary* conditions all resulted in higher scores than the *automatic (MMR) summary condition*. The difference is significant at $P=0.007$, $P=0.014$ and $P=0.012$ respectively. Although normality was assured, the Friedman Test further confirms a significant difference between conditions ($\chi^2(3)=11.684$, $P=0.009$).

4 F-measure

F-measure is an evaluation metric that balances precision and recall which has been used to evaluate summarization. Utterance level F-measure scores were calculated using the same summaries used in our human evaluation. In addition, three annotators were asked to create conventional gold standard summaries using binary selection. Annotators were not primed in any sense, did not watch the lecture videos, and had no sense of the higher level purpose of their annotations. We refer to the resulting summaries as context-free as they were not created under ecologically valid conditions. F-measure was also calculated with reference to these.

The F-measure results (Table 2) point out a few interesting phenomena. Firstly, when evaluating a given peer summary type with the same model type, the *generic-generic* scores are higher than both the *primed-primed* and *context-free-context-free* summaries. This means that generic summaries tend to share more utterances with each other, than primed summaries do, which are more varied. This seems unintuitive at first, but could potentially be explained by the possibility that different participants focused on different aspects of the priming quiz, due to either perceived importance, or lack of time (or summary space) to address all of the priming questions.

Peer Type	Model Type	Average F-measure
generic	*generic*	0.388
primed	*generic*	0.365
MMR	*generic*	0.214
generic	*primed*	0.365
primed	*primed*	0.374
MMR	*primed*	0.209
generic	*context-free*	0.371
primed	*context-free*	0.351
MMR	*context-free*	0.243
context-free	*context-free*	0.374

Table 2. Average F-measure

We also observe that generic summaries are more similar to conventionally annotated (context-free) summaries than either primed or MMR are. This makes sense and also confirms that even though primed summaries do not significantly outperform generic summaries in the quiz taking task, they are inherently distinguishable from each other.

Furthermore, when evaluating MMR using F-measure, we see that MMR summaries are most similar to the context-free summaries, whose utterance selections can be considered somewhat arbitrary. Our quiz results confirm MMR is significantly worse than generic and primed summaries. This casts doubt on the practice of using similarly annotated summaries as gold standards for summarization evaluation using ROUGE.

5 ROUGE Evaluation

More common than F-measure, ROUGE (Lin, 2004) is often used to evaluate summarization. Although Lin (2004) claimed to have demonstrated that ROUGE correlates well with human summaries, both Murray et al. (2005), and Liu and Liu (2010) have cast doubt upon this. It is important to acknowledge, however, that ROUGE is actually a family of measures, distinguished not only by the manner in which overlap is measured (1-grams, longest common subsequences, etc.), but by the provenience of the summaries that are provided to it as references. If these are not ecologically valid, there is no sense in holding ROUGE accountable for an erratic result.

To examine how ROUGE fairs under ecologically valid conditions, we calculated ROUGE-1, ROUGE-2, ROUGE-L, and ROUGE-SU4 on our data using the standard options outlined in previous DUC evaluations. ROUGE scores were calculated for each of the *generic manual summary*, *primed manual summary*, and *automatic summary* conditions. Each summary in a given condition was evaluated once against the *generic manual* summaries and once using the *primed manual* summaries. Similar to Liu and Liu (2010), ROUGE evaluation was conducted using leave-one-out on the model summary type and averaging the results.

In addition to calculating ROUGE on the summaries from our ecologically valid evaluation, we also followed more conventional ROUGE evaluation and used the same context-free annotator summaries as were used in our F-measure calculations above. Using these context-free summaries, the original generic manual, primed manual, and automatic summaries were evaluated using ROUGE. The result of these evaluations are presented in Table 3.

Looking at the ROUGE scores, we can see that when evaluated by each type of model summary, MMR performs worse than either generic or primed manual summaries. This is consistent with our quiz results, and perhaps shows that ROUGE may be able to distinguish human summaries from MMR. Looking at the *generic-generic*, *primed-primed*, and *context-free-context-free* scores, we can get a sense of how much agreement there was between summaries. It is not surprising that context-free annotator summaries showed the least agreement, as these summaries were generated with no higher purpose in mind. This suggests that using annotators to generate gold standards in such a manner is not ideal. In addition, real world applications for summarization would conceivably rarely consist of a situation where a summary was created for no apparent reason. More interesting is the observation that, when measured by ROUGE, primed summaries have less in common with each other than generic summaries do. The difference, however, is less pronounced when measured by ROUGE than by F-measure. This is likely due to the fact that ROUGE can account for semantically similar utterances.

Peer type	Model type	R-1	R-2	R-L	R-SU4
generic	*generic*	0.75461	0.48439	0.75151	0.51547
primed	*generic*	0.74408	0.46390	0.74097	0.49806
MMR	*generic*	0.71659	0.40176	0.71226	0.44838
generic	*primed*	0.74457	0.46432	0.74091	0.49844
primed	*primed*	0.74693	0.46977	0.74344	0.50254
MMR	*primed*	0.70773	0.38874	0.70298	0.43802
generic	*context-free*	0.72735	0.46421	0.72432	0.49573
primed	*context-free*	0.71793	0.44325	0.71472	0.47805
MMR	*context-free*	0.69233	0.37600	0.68813	0.42413
context-free	*context-free*	0.70707	0.44897	0.70365	0.48019

Table 3. Average ROUGE Scores

5.1 Correlation with Quiz Scores

In order to assess the ability of ROUGE to predict quiz scores, we measured the correlation between ROUGE scores and quiz scores on a per participant basis. Similar to Murray et al. (2005), and Liu and Liu (2010), we used Spearman's rank coefficient (rho) to measure the correlation between ROUGE and our human evaluation. Correlation was measured both by calculating Spearman's rho on all data points ("all" in Table 4) and by performing the calculation separately for each lecture and averaging the results ("avg"). Significant rho values (p-value less than 0.05) are shown in bold.

Note that there are not many bolded values, indicating that there are few (anti-)correlations between quiz scores and ROUGE. The rho values reported by Liu and Liu (2010) correspond to the "all" row of our generic-context-free scores (Liu and Liu (2010) did not report ROUGE-L), and we obtained roughly the same scores as they did. In contrast to this, our "all" generic-generic correlations are very low. It is possible that the lectures condition the parameters of the correlation to such an extent that fitting all of the quiz-ROUGE pairs to the same correlation across lectures is unreasonable. It may therefore be more useful to look at rho values computed by lecture. For these values, our R-SU4 scores are not as high relative to R-1 and R-2 as those reported by Liu and Liu (2010). It is also worth noting that the use of context-free binary selections as a reference results in increased correlation for generic summaries, but substantially decreases correlation for primed summaries.

With the exception that generic references prefer generic summaries and primed references prefer primed summaries, all other values indicate that both generic and primed summaries are better than MMR. However, instead of ranking summary types, what is important here is the ecologically valid quiz scores. Our data provides no evidence that ROUGE scores accurately predict quiz scores.

6 Conclusions

We have presented an investigation into how current measures and methodologies for evaluating summarization systems compare to human-centric evaluation criteria. An ecologically-valid evaluation was conducted that determines the value of a summary when embedded in a task, rather than how closely a summary resembles a gold standard. The resulting quiz scores indicate that manual summaries are significantly better than MMR. ROUGE scores were calculated using the summaries created in the study. In addition, more conventional context-free annotator summaries were also used in ROUGE evaluation. Spearman's rho indicated no correlation between ROUGE scores and our ecologically valid quiz scores. The results offer evidence that ROUGE scores and particularly context-free annotator-generated summaries as gold standards may not always be reliably used in place of an ecologically valid evaluation.

Peer type	Model type		R-1	R-2	R-L	R-SU4
generic	*generic*	all	0.017	0.066	0.005	0.058
		lec1	0.236	0.208	0.229	0.208
		lec2	0.276	0.28	0.251	0.092
		lec3	0.307	**0.636**	0.269	0.428
		lec4	0.193	-0.011	0.175	0.018
		avg	0.253	0.278	0.231	0.187
primed	*generic*	all	-0.097	-0.209	-0.090	-0.192
		lec1	-0.239	-0.458	-0.194	-0.458
		lec2	-0.306	-0.281	-0.306	-0.316
		lec3	0.191	0.142	0.116	0.255
		lec4	**-0.734**	**-0.78**	**-0.769**	**-0.78**
		avg	-0.272	-0.344	-0.288	-0.325
generic	*primed*	all	0.009	0.158	-0.004	0.133
		lec1	0.367	0.247	0.367	0.162
		lec2	**0.648**	0.425	**0.634**	0.304
		lec3	0.078	0.417	0.028	0.382
		lec4	0.129	0.079	0.115	0.025
		avg	0.306	0.292	0.286	0.218
primed	*primed*	all	0.161	0.042	0.161	0.045
		lec1	0.042	-0.081	0.042	-0.194
		lec2	0.238	0.284	0.259	0.284
		lec3	0.205	0.12	0.205	0.12
		lec4	0.226	0.423	0.314	0.423
		avg	0.178	0.187	0.205	0.158
generic	*con-text-free*	all	0.282	**0.306**	0.265	**0.347**
		lec1	-0.067	0.296	-0.004	0.325
		lec2	0.414	0.414	0.438	0.319
		lec3	0.41	0.555	0.41	0.555
		lec4	0.136	0.007	0.136	0.054
		avg	0.223	0.318	0.245	0.313
primed	*con-text-free*	all	-0.146	-0.282	-0.151	**-0.305**
		lec1	0.151	-0.275	0.151	-0.299
		lec2	-0.366	**-0.611**	-0.366	**-0.636**
		lec3	0.273	0.212	0.273	0.202
		lec4	**-0.815**	-0.677	**-0.825**	**-0.755**
		avg	-0.189	-0.338	-0.192	-0.372

Table 4. Correlation (Spearman's rho) between Quiz Scores and ROUGE

7 References

J. Carbonell and J. Goldstein. 1998. The use of mmr, diversity-based reranking for reordering documents and producing summaries. In *Proceedings of the 21st annual international ACM SIGIR conference on Research and development in information retrieval*, 335-336, ACM.

P. R. Cohen. 1995. *Empirical methods for artificial intelligence*. Volume 55. MIT press Cambridge, Massachusetts.

H. Christensen, B. Kolluru, Y. Gotoh, and S. Renals. 2004. From text summarisation to style-specific summarisation for broadcast news. *Advances in Information Retrieval*, 223-237.

L. He, E. Sanocki, A. Gupta, and J. Grudin. 1999. Auto-summarization of audio-video presentations. In *Proceedings of the seventh ACM international conference on Multimedia (Part 1)*, 489-498. ACM.

L. He, E. Sanocki, A. Gupta, and J. Grudin. 2000. Comparing presentation summaries: slides vs. reading vs. listening. In *Proc. of the SIGCHI*, 177-184, ACM.

C. Lin. 2004. Rouge: a package for automatic evaluation of summaries. In *Proc. of ACL, Text Summarization Branches Out Workshop*, 74–81.

F. Liu and Y. Liu. 2010. Exploring correlation between rouge and human evaluation on meeting summaries. *Audio, Speech, and Language Processing, IEEE Transactions on*, 18(1):187-196.

C. Munteanu, R. Baecker, G. Penn, E. Toms, and D. James. 2006. The effect of speech recognition accuracy rates on the usefulness and usability of webcast archives. In *Proceedings of the SIGCHI conference on Human Factors in computing systems*, 493-502, ACM.

G. Murray, S. Renals, J. Carletta, and J. Moore. 2005. Evaluating automatic summaries of meeting recordings. In *Proc. of the ACL 2005 MTSE Workshop*, Ann Arbor, MI, USA, 33-40.

G. Murray, T. Kleinbauer, P. Poller, S. Renals, J. Kilgour, and T. Becker. 2008. Extrinsic summarization evaluation: A decision audit task. *Machine Learning for Multimodal Interaction*, 349-361.

G. Penn and X. Zhu. 2008. A critical reassessment of evaluation baselines for speech summarization. *Proc. of ACL-HLT*.

S. Tucker, O. Bergman, A. Ramamoorthy, and S. Whittaker. 2010. Catchup: a useful application of time-travel in meetings. In *Proc. of CSCW*, 99-102, ACM.

S. Tucker and S. Whittaker. 2006. Time is of the essence: an evaluation of temporal compression algorithms. In *Proc. of the SIGCHI*, 329-338, ACM.

The Heterogeneity Principle in Evaluation Measures for Automatic Summarization*

Enrique Amigó Julio Gonzalo Felisa Verdejo
UNED, Madrid
{enrique,julio,felisa}@lsi.uned.es

Abstract

The development of summarization systems requires reliable similarity (evaluation) measures that compare system outputs with human references. A reliable measure should have correspondence with human judgements. However, the reliability of measures depends on the test collection in which the measure is meta-evaluated; for this reason, it has not yet been possible to reliably establish which are the best evaluation measures for automatic summarization. In this paper, we propose an unsupervised method called Heterogeneity-Based Ranking (HBR) that combines summarization evaluation measures without requiring human assessments. Our empirical results indicate that HBR achieves a similar correspondence with human assessments than the best single measure for every observed corpus. In addition, HBR results are more robust across topics than single measures.

1 Introduction

In general, automatic evaluation metrics for summarization are similarity measures that compare system outputs with human references. The typical development cycle of a summarization system begins with selecting the most predictive metric. For this, evaluation metrics are compared to each other in terms of correlation with human judgements. The second step consists of tuning the summarization system (typically in several iterations) in order to maximize the scores according to the selected evaluation measure.

There is a wide set of available measures beyond the standard ROUGE: for instance, those comparing basic linguistic elements (Hovy et al., 2005), dependency triples (Owczarzak, 2009) or convolution kernels (Hirao et al., 2005) which reported some reliability improvement with respect to ROUGE in terms of correlation with human judgements. However, in practice ROUGE is still the preferred metric of choice. The main reason is that the superiority of a measure with respect to other is not easy to demonstrate: the variability of results across corpora, reference judgements (Pyramid vs responsiveness) and correlation criteria (system vs. summary level) is substantial. In the absence of a clear quality criterion, the de-facto standard is usually the most reasonable choice.

In this paper we rethink the development cycle of summarization systems. Given that the best measure changes across evaluation scenarios, we propose using multiple automatic evaluation measures, together with an unsupervised method to combine measures called *Heterogeneity Based Ranking* (HBR). This method is grounded on the general Heterogeneity property proposed in (Amigó et al., 2011), which states that the more a measure set is heterogeneous, the more a score increase according to all the measures simultaneously is reliable. In brief, the HBR method consists of computing the heterogeneity of measures for which a

*This work has been partially funded by the Madrid government, grant MA2VICMR (S-2009/TIC- 1542), the Spanish Government, grant Holopedia (TIN2010-21128-C02-01) and the European Community's Seventh Framework Programme (FP7/ 2007-2013) under grant agreement nr. 288024 (LiMoSINe project).

system-produced summary improves each of the rest of summaries in comparison.

Our empirical results indicate that HBR achieves a similar correspondence with human assessments than the best single measure for every observed corpus. In addition, HBR results are more robust across topics than single measures.

2 Definitions

We consider here the definition of similarity measure proposed in (Amigó et al., 2011):

Being Ω the universe of system outputs (summaries) s and gold-standards (human references) g, we assume that a similarity measure is a function $x : \Omega^2 \longrightarrow \Re$ such that there exists a decomposition function $f : \Omega \longrightarrow \{e_1..e_n\}$ (e.g., words or other linguistic units or relationships) satisfying the following constraints; (i) maximum similarity is achieved only when the summary decomposition resembles exactly the gold standard; (ii) adding one element from the gold standard increases the similarity; and (iii) removing one element that does not appear in the gold standard also increases the similarity. Formally:

$$f(s) = f(g) \Longleftrightarrow x(s,g) = 1$$

$$(f(s) = f(s') \cup \{e_g \in f(g) \setminus f(s)\}) \Longrightarrow x(s,g) > x(s',g)$$

$$(f(s) = f(s') - \{e_{\neg g} \in f(s) \setminus f(g)\}) \Longrightarrow x(s,g) > x(s',g)$$

This definition excludes random functions, or the inverse of any similarity function (e.g. $\frac{1}{f(s)}$). It covers, however, any overlapping or precision/recall measure over words, n-grams, syntactic structures or any kind of semantic unit. In the rest of the paper, given that the gold standard g in summary evaluation is usually fixed, we will simplify the notation saying that $x(s,g) \equiv x(s)$.

We consider also the definition of *heterogeneity* of a measure set proposed in (Amigó et al., 2011):

The heterogeneity $H(\mathcal{X})$ of a set of measures $\mathcal{X}$ is defined as, given two summaries s and s' such that $g \neq s \neq s' \neq g$ (g is the reference text), the probability that there exists two measures that contradict each other.

$$H(\mathcal{X}) \equiv P_{s,s' \neq g}(\exists x, x' \in \mathcal{X} / x(s) > x(s') \wedge x'(s) < x'(s'))$$

3 Proposal

The proposal in this paper is grounded on the heterogeneity property of evaluation measures introduced in (Amigó et al., 2011). This property establishes a relationship between heterogeneity and reliability of measures. However, this work does not provide any method to evaluate and rank summaries given a set of available automatic evaluation measures. We now reformulate the heterogeneity property in order to define a method to combine measures and rank systems.

3.1 Heterogeneity Property Reformulation

The heterogeneity property of evaluation measures introduced in (Amigó et al., 2011) states that, assuming that measures are based on similarity to human references, the real quality difference between two texts is lower bounded by the heterogeneity of measures that corroborate the quality increase. We reformulate this property in the following way:

Given a set of automatic evaluation measures based on similarity to human references, the probability of a quality increase in summaries is correlated with the heterogeneity of the set of measures that corroborate this increase:

$$P(Q(s) \geq Q(s')) \sim H(\{x | x(s) \geq x(s')\})$$

where $Q(s)$ is the quality of the summary s according to human assessments. In addition, the probability is maximal if the heterogeneity is maximal:

$$H(\{x | x(s) \geq x(s')\}) = 1 \Rightarrow P(Q(s) \geq Q(s')) = 1$$

The first part is derived from the fact that increasing heterogeneity requires additional diverse measures corroborating the similarity increase ($H(\{x|x(s) \geq x(s')\})$)). The correlation is the result of assuming that a similarity increase according to any aspect is always a positive evidence of true similarity to human references. In other words, a positive match between the automatic summary and the human references, according to any feature, should never be a negative evidence of quality.

As for the second part, if the heterogeneity of a measure set X is maximal, then the condition of the heterogeneity definition ($\exists x, x' \in \mathcal{X}. x(s) > x(s') \wedge x'(s) < x'(s')$) holds for any pair of summaries that are different from the human references. Given that all measures in X corroborate the similarity increase ($X = \{x | x(s) \geq x(s')\}$), the heterogeneity condition does not hold. Then, at least one of the evaluated summaries is not different from the human reference and we can ensure that $P(Q(s) \geq Q(s')) = 1$.

3.2 The Heterogeneity Based Ranking

The main goal in summarization evaluation is ranking systems according to their quality. This can be seen as estimating, for each system-produced summary s, the average probability of being "better" than other summaries:

$$\text{Rank}(s) = \text{Avg}_{s'}(P(Q(s) \geq Q(s')))$$

Applying the reformulated heterogeneity property we can estimate this as:

$$\text{HBR}_{\mathcal{X}}(s) = \text{Avg}_{s'}(H(\{x | x(s) \geq x(s')\}))$$

We refer to this ranking function as the *Heterogeneity Based Ranking* (HBR). It satisfies three crucial properties for a measure combining function. Note that, assuming that any similarity measure over human references represents a positive evidence of quality, the measure combining function must be at least robust with respect to redundant or random measures:

1. HBR is independent from measure scales and it does not require relative weighting schemes between measures. Formally, being f any strict growing function:

$$\text{HBR}_{x_1..x_n}(s) = \text{HBR}_{x_1..f(x_n)}(s)$$

2. HBR is not sensitive to redundant measures:

$$\text{HBR}_{x_1..x_n}(s) = \text{HBR}_{x_1..x_n,x_n}(s)$$

3. Given a large enough set of similarity instances, HBR is not sensitive to non-informative measures. In other words, being x_r a random function such that $P(x_r(s) > x_r(s')) = \frac{1}{2}$, then:

$$\text{HBR}_{x_1..x_n}(s) \sim \text{HBR}_{x_1..x_n,x_r}(s)$$

The first two properties are trivially satisfied: the $\exists$ operator in H and the score comparisons are not affected by redundant measures nor their scale properties. Regarding the third property, the Heterogeneity of a set of measures plus a random function x_r is:

$$H(\mathcal{X} \cup \{x_r\}) \equiv$$

$$P_{s,s'}(\exists x, x' \in \mathcal{X} \cup \{x_r\} | x(s) > x(s') \wedge x'(s) < x'(s')) =$$

$$H(\mathcal{X}) + (1 - H(\mathcal{X})) * \frac{1}{2} = \frac{H(\mathcal{X}) + 1}{2}$$

That is, the Heterogeneity grows proportionally when including a random function. Assuming that the random function corroborates the similarity increase in a half of cases, the result is a proportional relationship between HBR and HBR with the additional measure. Note that we need to assume a large enough amount of data to avoid random effects.

4 Experimental Setting

4.1 Test Bed

We have used the AS test collections used in the DUC 2005 and DUC 2006 evaluation campaigns[1] (Dang, 2005; Dang, 2006). The task was to generate a question focused summary of 250 words from a set of 25-50 documents to a complex question. Summaries were evaluated according to several criteria. Here, we will consider the responsiveness judgements, in which the quality score was an integer between 1 and 5. See Table 1 for a brief numerical description of these test beds.

In order to check the measure combining method, we have employed standard variants of ROUGE (Lin, 2004), including the reversed precision version for each variant [2]. We have considered also the F

[1] http://duc.nist.gov/

[2] Note that the original ROUGE measures are oriented to recall

	DUC 2005	DUC 2006
#human-references	3-4	3-4
#systems	32	35
#system-outputs-assessed	32	35
#system-outputs	50	50
#outputs-assessed per-system	50	50

Table 1: Test collections from 2005 and 2006 DUC evaluation campaigns used in our experiments.

measure between recall and precision oriented measures. Finally, our measure set includes also BE or Basic Elements (Hovy et al., 2006).

4.2 Meta-evaluation criterion

The traditional way of meta-evaluating measures consists of computing the Pearson correlation between measure scores and quality human assessments. But the main goal of automatic evaluation metrics is not exactly to predict the real quality of systems; rather than this, their core mission is detecting system outputs that improve the baseline system in each development cycle. Therefore, the issue is to what extent a quality increase between two system outputs is reflected by the output ranking produced by the measure.

According to this perspective, we propose meta-evaluating measures in terms of an extended version of AUC (Area Under the Curve). AUC can be seen as the probability of observing a score increase when observing a real quality increase between two system outputs (Fawcett, 2006).

$$AUC(x) = P(x(s) > x(s')|Q(s) > Q(s'))$$

In order to customize this measure to our scenario, two special cases must be handled:

(i) For cases in which both summaries obtain the same value, we assume that the measure rewards each instance with equal probability. That is, if $x(s) = x(s')$,$P(x(s) > x(s')|Q(s) > Q(s')) = \frac{1}{2}$.

(ii) Given that in the AS evaluation scenarios there are multiple quality levels, we still apply the same probabilistic AUC definition, considering pairs of summaries in which one of them achieves more quality than the other according to human assessors.

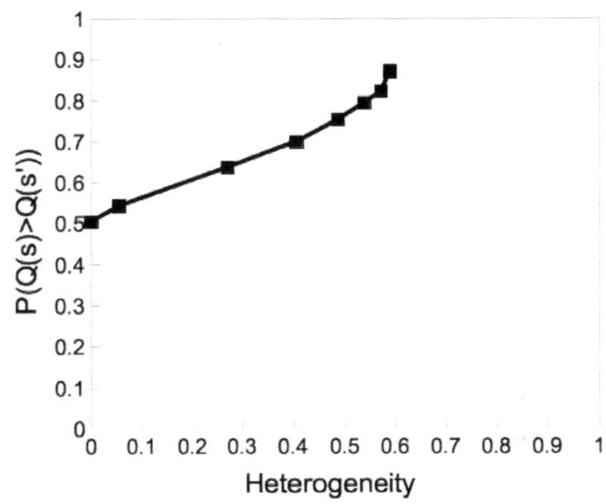

Figure 1: Correlation between probability of quality increase and Heterogeneity of measures that corroborate the increase

5 Experiments

5.1 Measure Heterogeneity vs. Quality Increase

We hypothesize that the probability of a real similarity increase to human references (as stated by human assessments) is directly related to the heterogeneity of the set of measures that confirm such increase. In order to verify whether this principle holds in practice, we need to measure the correlation between both variables. Therefore, we compute, for each pair of summaries in the same topic the heterogeneity of the set of measures that corroborate a score increase between both:

$$H(\{x \in \mathcal{X} | x(s) \geq x(s')\})$$

The Heterogeneity has been estimated by counting cases over 10,000 samples (pairs of summaries) in both corpora.

Then, we have sorted each pair $\langle s, s' \rangle$ according to its related heterogeneity. We have divided the resulting rank in 100 intervals of the same size. For

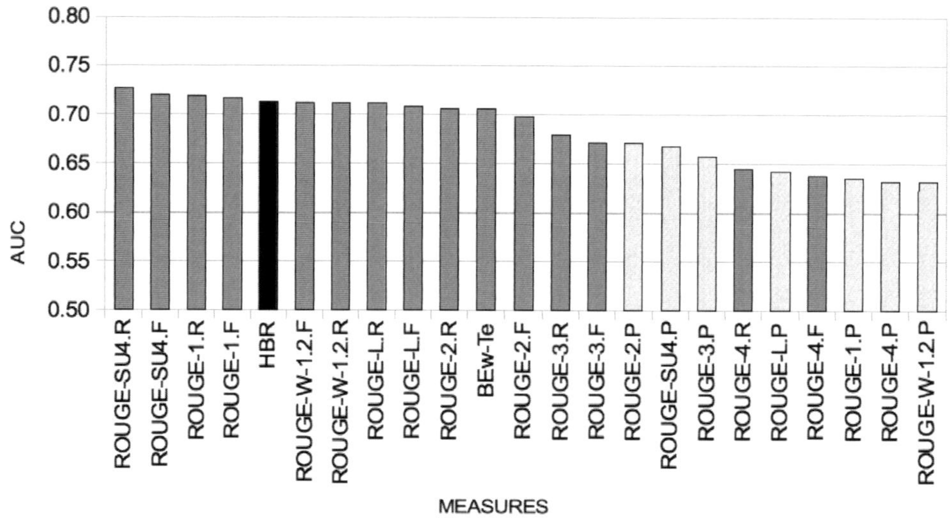

Figure 2: AUC comparison between HBR and single measures in DUC 2005 and DUC 2006 corpora.

each interval, we have computed the average heterogeneity of the set and the probability of real quality increase $(P(Q(s) \geq Q(s')))$.

Figure 1 displays the results. Note that the direct relation between both variables is clear: a key for predicting a real quality increase is how heterogeneous is the set of measures corroborating it.

5.2 HBR vs. Single Measures

In the following experiment, we compute HBR and we compare the resulting AUC with that of single measures. The heterogeneity of measures is estimated over samples in both corpora (DUC 2005 and DUC 2006), and HBR ranking is computed to rank summaries for each topic. For the meta-evaluation, the AUC probability is computed over summary pairs from the same topic.

Figure 2 shows the resulting AUC values of single measures and HBR. The black bar represents the HBR approach. The light grey bars are ROUGE measures oriented to precision. The dark grey bars include ROUGE variants oriented to recall and F, and the measure BE. As the Figure shows, recall-based measures achieve in general higher AUC values than precision-oriented measures. The HBR measure combination appears near the top. It is improved by some measures such as ROUGE_SU4_R, although the difference is not statistically significant ($p = 0.36$ for a t-test between ROUGE_SU4_R and HBR, for instance). HBR improves the 10 worst single measures with statistical significance ($p < 0.025$).

5.3 Robustness

The next question is why using HBR instead of the "best" measure (ROUGE-SU4-R in this case). As we mentioned, the reliability of measures can vary across scenarios. For instance, in DUC scenarios most systems are extractive, and exploit the maximum size allowed in the evaluation campaign guidelines. Therefore, the precision over long n-grams is not crucial, given that the grammaticality of summaries is ensured. In this scenario the recall over words or short n-grams over human references is a clear signal of quality. But we can not ensure that these characteristics will be kept in other corpora, or even when evaluating new kind of summarizers with the same corpora.

Our hypothesis is that, given that HBR resembles the best measure without using human assessments, it should have a more stable performance in situations where the best measure changes.

In order to check empirically this assertion, we have investigated the lower bound performance of measures in our test collections. First, we have ranked measures for each topic according to their AUC values; Then, we have computed, for every measure, its rank regarding the rest of measures (scaled from 0 to 1). Finally, we average each measure across the 10% of topics in which the measure

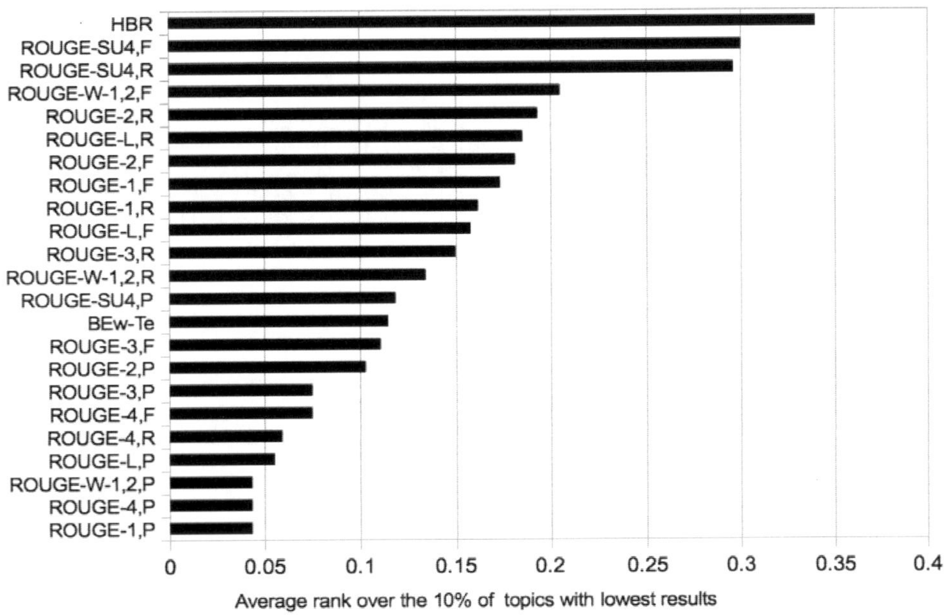

Figure 3: Average rank of measures over the 10% of topics with lowest results for the measure.

gets the worst ranks. Figure 3 shows the results: the worst performance of HBR across topics is better than the worst performance of any single measure. This confirms that the combination of measures using HBR is indeed more robust than any measure in isolation.

5.4 Consistent vs. Inconsistent Topics

The Heterogeneity property is grounded on the assumption that any similarity criteria represents a positive evidence of similarity to human references. In general, we can assert that this assumption holds over a large enough random set of texts. However, depending on the distribution of summaries in the corpus, this assumption may not always hold. For instance, we can assume that, given all possible summaries, improving the word precision with respect to the gold standard can never be a negative evidence of quality. However, for a certain topic, it could happen that the worst summaries are also the shortest, and have high precision and low recall. In this case, precision-based similarity could be correlated with negative quality. Let us refer to these as *inconsistent* topics vs. *consistent* topics. In terms of AUC, a measure represents a negative evidence of quality when AUC is lower than 0.5. Our test collections contain 100 topics, out of which 25 are inconsistent (i.e., at least one measure achieves AUC values lower than 0.5) and 75 are consistent with respect to our measure set (all measures achieve AUC values higher than 0.5).

Figure **??** illustrates the AUC achieved by measures when inconsistent topics are excluded. As with the full set of topics, recall-based measures achieve higher AUC values than precision-based measures; but, in this case, HBR appears at the top of the ranking. This result illustrates that (i) HBR behaves particularly well when our assumptions on similarity measures hold in the corpus; and that (ii) in practice, there may be topics for which our assumptions do not hold.

6 Conclusions

In this paper, we have confirmed that the heterogeneity of a set of summary evaluation measures is correlated with the probability of finding a real quality improvement when all measures corroborate it. The HBR measure combination method is based on this principle, which is grounded on the assumption that any similarity increase with respect to human references is a positive signal of quality.

Our empirical results indicate that the Heterogeneity Based Ranking achieves a reliability similar to the best single measure in the set. In addi-

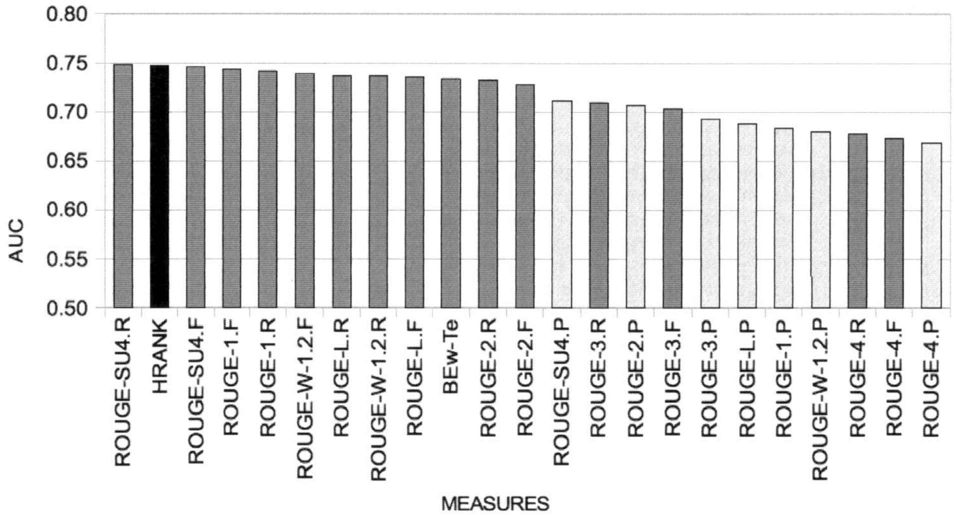

Figure 4: AUC comparison between HBR and single measures in corpora DUC2005 and DUC 2006 over topics in which all measures achieve AUC bigger than 0.5.

tion, HBR results are more robust across topics than single measures. Our experiments also suggest that HBR behaves particularly well when the assumptions of the heterogeneity property holds in the corpus. These assumptions are conditioned by the distribution of summaries in the corpus (in particular, on the amount and variability of the summaries that are compared with human references), and in practice 25% of the topics in our test collections do not satisfy them for our set of measures.

The HBR (Heterogeneity Based Ranking) method proposed in this paper does not represent the "best automatic evaluation measure". Rather than this, it promotes the development of new measures. What HBR does is solving –or at least palliating– the problem of reliability variance of measures across test beds. According to our analysis, our practical recommendations for system refinement are:

1. Compile an heterogenous set of measures, covering multiple linguistic aspects (such as n-gram precision, recall, basic linguistic structures, etc.).

2. Considering the summarization scenario, discard measures that might not always represent a positive evidence of quality. For instance, if very short summaries are allowed (e.g. one word) and they are very frequent in the set of system outputs to be compared to each other, precision oriented measures may violate HBR assumptions.

3. Evaluate automatically your new summarization approach within this corpus according to the HBR method.

Our priority for future work is now developing a reference benchmark containing an heterogenous set of summaries, human references and measures satisfying the heterogeneity assumptions and covering multiple summarization scenarios where different measures play different roles.

The HBR software is available at http://nlp.uned.es/∼enrique/

References

Enrique Amigó, Julio Gonzalo, Jesus Gimenez, and Felisa Verdejo. 2011. Corroborating text evaluation results with heterogeneous measures. In *Proceedings of the 2011 Conference on Empirical Methods in Natural Language Processing*, pages 455–466, Edinburgh, Scotland, UK., July. Association for Computational Linguistics.

Hoa Trang Dang. 2005. Overview of DUC 2005. In *Proceedings of the 2005 Document Understanding Workshop*.

Hoa Trang Dang. 2006. Overview of DUC 2006. In *Proceedings of the 2006 Document Understanding Workshop*.

Tom Fawcett. 2006. An introduction to roc analysis. *Pattern Recogn. Lett.*, 27:861–874, June.

Tsutomu Hirao, Manabu Okumura, and Hideki Isozaki. 2005. Kernel-based approach for automatic evaluation of natural language generation technologies: Application to automatic summarization. In *Proceedings of Human Language Technology Conference and Conference on Empirical Methods in Natural Language Processing*, pages 145–152, Vancouver, British Columbia, Canada, October. Association for Computational Linguistics.

Eduard Hovy, Chin-Yew Lin, and Liang Zhou. 2005. Evaluating DUC 2005 using Basic Elements. Proceedings of Document Understanding Conference (DUC). Vancouver, B.C., Canada.

Eduard Hovy, Chin-Yew Lin, Liang Zhou, and Junichi Fukumoto. 2006. Automated Summarization Evaluation with Basic Elements. In *Proceedings of the 5th International Conference on Language Resources and Evaluation (LREC)*, pages 899–902.

Chin-Yew Lin. 2004. Rouge: A Package for Automatic Evaluation of Summaries. In Marie-Francine Moens and Stan Szpakowicz, editors, *Text Summarization Branches Out: Proceedings of the ACL-04 Workshop*, pages 74–81, Barcelona, Spain, July. Association for Computational Linguistics.

Karolina Owczarzak. 2009. Depeval(summ): dependency-based evaluation for automatic summaries. In *ACL-IJCNLP '09: Proceedings of the Joint Conference of the 47th Annual Meeting of the ACL and the 4th International Joint Conference on Natural Language Processing of the AFNLP: Volume 1*, pages 190–198, Morristown, NJ, USA. Association for Computational Linguistics.

Discrepancy Between Automatic and Manual Evaluation of Summaries

Shamima Mithun, Leila Kosseim, and Prasad Perera
Concordia University
Department of Computer Science and Software Engineering
Montreal, Quebec, Canada
{s_mithun, kosseim, p_perer}@encs.concordia.ca

Abstract

Today, automatic evaluation metrics such as ROUGE have become the de-facto mode of evaluating an automatic summarization system. However, based on the DUC and the TAC evaluation results, (Conroy and Schlesinger, 2008; Dang and Owczarzak, 2008) showed that the performance gap between human-generated summaries and system-generated summaries is clearly visible in manual evaluations but is often not reflected in automated evaluations using ROUGE scores. In this paper, we present our own experiments in comparing the results of manual evaluations versus automatic evaluations using our own text summarizer: BlogSum. We have evaluated BlogSum-generated summary content using ROUGE and compared the results with the original candidate list (OList). The t-test results showed that there is no significant difference between BlogSum-generated summaries and OList summaries. However, two manual evaluations for content using two different datasets show that BlogSum performed significantly better than OList. A manual evaluation of summary coherence also shows that BlogSum performs significantly better than OList. These results agree with previous work and show the need for a better automated summary evaluation metric rather than the standard ROUGE metric.

1 Introduction

Today, any NLP task must be accompanied by a well-accepted evaluation scheme. This is why, for the last 15 years, to evaluate automated summarization systems, sets of evaluation data (corpora, topics, ...) and baselines have been established in text summarization competitions such as TREC[1], DUC[2], and TAC[3]. Although evaluation is essential to verify the quality of a summary or to compare different summarization approaches, the evaluation criteria used are by no means universally accepted (Das and Martins, 2007). Summary evaluation is a difficult task because no ideal summary is available for a set of input documents. In addition, it is also difficult to compare different summaries and establish a baseline because of the absence of standard human or automatic summary evaluation metrics. On the other hand, manual evaluation is very expensive. According to (Lin, 2004), large scale manual evaluations of all participants' summaries in the DUC 2003 conference would require over 3000 hours of human efforts to evaluate summary content and linguistic qualities.

The goal of this paper is to show that the literature and our own work empirically point out the need for a better automated summary evaluation metric rather than the standard ROUGE metric[4] (Lin, 2004).

2 Current Evaluation Schemes

The available summary evaluation techniques can be divided into two categories: manual and automatic. To do a manual evaluation, human experts assess different qualities of the system generated summaries. On the other hand, for an automatic eval-

[1]Text REtrieval Conference: http://trec.nist.gov
[2]Document Understanding Conference: http://duc.nist.gov
[3]Text Analysis Conference: http://www.nist.gov/tac
[4]http://berouge.com/default.aspx

uation, tools are used to compare the system generated summaries with human generated gold standard summaries or reference summaries. Although they are faster to perform and result in consistent evaluations, automatic evaluations can only address superficial concepts such as n-grams matching, because many required qualities such as coherence and grammaticality cannot be measured automatically. As a result, human judges are often called for to evaluate or cross check the quality of the summaries, but in many cases human judges have different opinions. Hence inter-annotator agreement is often computed as well.

The quality of a summary is assessed mostly on its content and linguistic quality (Louis and Nenkova, 2008). Content evaluation of a query-based summary is performed based on the relevance with the topic and the question and the inclusion of important contents from the input documents. The linguistic quality of a summary is evaluated manually based on how it structures and presents the contents. Mainly, subjective evaluation is done to assess the linguistic quality of an automatically generated summary. Grammaticality, non-redundancy, referential clarity, focus, structure and coherence are commonly used factors considered to evaluate the linguistic quality. A study by (Das and Martins, 2007) shows that evaluating the content of a summary is more difficult compared to evaluating its linguistic quality.

There exist different measures to evaluate an output summary. The most commonly used metrics are *recall*, *precision*, *F-measure*, *Pyramid score*, and *ROUGE/BE*.

Automatic versus Manual Evaluation

Based on an analysis of the 2005-2007 DUC data, (Conroy and Schlesinger, 2008) showed that the ROUGE evaluation and a human evaluation can significantly vary due to the fact that ROUGE ignores linguistic quality of summaries, which has a huge influence in human evaluation. (Dang and Owczarzak, 2008) also pointed out that automatic evaluation is rather different than the one based on manual assessment. They explained this the following way: "automatic metrics, based on string matching, are unable to appreciate a summary that uses different phrases than the reference text, even if such a summary is perfectly fine by human standards".

To evaluate both opinionated and news article based summarization approaches, previously mentioned evaluation metrics such as ROUGE or Pyramid are used. Shared evaluation tasks such as DUC and TAC competitions also use these methods to evaluate participants' summary. Table 1 shows

Table 1: Human and Automatic System Performance at Various TAC Competitions

	Model (Human)		**Automatic**	
	Pyr.	**Resp.**	**Pyr.**	**Resp.**
2010 Upd.	0.78	4.76	0.30	2.56
2009 Upd.	0.68	8.83	0.26	4.14
2008 Upd.	0.66	4.62	0.26	2.32
2008 Opi.	0.44	Unk.	0.10	1.31

the evaluation results of automatic systems' average performance at the TAC 2008 to 2010 conferences using the pyramid score (Pyr.) and responsiveness (Resp.). In this evaluation, the pyramid score was used to calculate the content relevance and the responsiveness of a summary was used to judge the overall quality or usefulness of the summary, considering both the information content and linguistic quality. These two criteria were evaluated manually. The pyramid score was calculated out of 1 and the responsiveness measures were calculated on a scale of 1 to 5 (1, being the worst). However, in 2009, responsiveness was calculated on a scale of 10. Table 1 also shows a comparison between automatic systems and human participants (model). In Table 1, the first 3 rows show the evaluation results of the TAC Update Summarization (Upd.) initial summary generation task (which were generated for news articles) and the last row shows the evaluation results of the TAC 2008 Opinion Summarization track (Opi.) where summaries were generated from blogs. From Table 1, we can see that in both criteria, automatic systems are weaker than humans. (Note that in the table, Unk. refers to unknown.)

Interestingly, in an automatic evaluation, often, not only is there no significant gap between models and systems, but in many cases, automatic systems scored higher than some human models.

Table 2 shows the performance of human (H.) and automated systems (S.) (participants) using automated and manual evaluation in the TAC 2008 up-

Table 2: Automated vs. Manual Evaluation at TAC 2008

	Automated		Manual		
	R-2	**R-SU4**	**Pyr.**	**Ling.**	**Resp.**
H. Mean	0.12	0.15	0.66	4.79	4.62
S. Mean	0.08	0.12	0.26	2.33	2.32
H. Best	0.13	0.17	0.85	4.91	4.79
S. Best	0.11	0.14	0.36	3.25	2.29

date summarization track. In the table, R-2 and R-SU4 refer to ROUGE-2 and ROUGE-SU4 and Pyr., Ling., and Resp. refer to Pyramid, linguistic, and responsiveness, respectively. A *t*-test of statistical significance applied to the data in Table 2 shows that there is no significant difference between human and participants in automated evaluation but that there is a significant performance difference between them in the manual evaluation.

These findings indicate that ROUGE is not the most effective tool to evaluate summaries. Our own experiments described below arrive at the same conclusion.

3 BlogSum

We have designed an extractive query-based summrizer called BlogSum. In BlogSum, we have developed our own sentence extractor to retrieve the initial list of candidate sentences (we called it OList) based on question similarity, topic similarity, and subjectivity scores. Given a set of initial candidate sentences, BlogSum generates summaries using discourse relations within a schema-based framework. Details of BlogSum is outside the scope of this paper. For details, please see (Mithun and Kosseim, 2011).

4 Evaluation of BlogSum

BlogSum-generated summaries have been evaluated for content and linguistic quality, specifically discourse coherence. The evaluation of the content was done both automatically and manually and the evaluation of the coherence was done manually. Our evaluation results also reflect the discrepancy between automatic and manual evaluation schemes of summaries described above.

In our evaluation, BlogSum-generated summaries were compared with the original candidate list generated by our approach without the discourse re-ordering (OList). However, we have validated our original candidate list with a publicly available sentence ranker. Specifically, we have conducted an experiment to verify whether MEAD-generated summaries (Radev et al., 2004), a widely used publicly available summarizer[5], were better than our candidate list (OList). In this evaluation, we have generated summaries using MEAD with centroid, query title, and query narrative features. In MEAD, query title and query narrative features are implemented using cosine similarity based on the *tf-idf* value. In this evaluation, we used the TAC 2008 opinion summarization dataset (described later in this section) and summaries were evaluated using the ROUGE-2 and ROUGE-SU4 scores. Table 3 shows the results of the automatic evaluation using ROUGE based on summary content.

Table 3: Automatic Evaluation of MEAD based on Summary Content on TAC 2008

System	R-2 (F)	R-SU4 (F)
MEAD	0.0407	0.0642
Average	0.0690	0.0860
OList	0.1020	0.1070

Table 3 shows that MEAD-generated summaries achieved weaker ROUGE scores compared to that of our candidate list (OList). The table also shows that MEAD performs weaker than the average performance of the participants of TAC 2008 (Average). We suspect that these poor results are due to several reasons. First, in MEAD, we cannot use opinionated terms or polarity information as a sentence selection feature. On the other hand, most of the summarizers, which deal with opinionated texts, use opinionated terms and polarity information for this purpose. In addition, in this experiment, for some of the TAC 2008 questions, MEAD was unable to create any summary. This evaluation results prompted us to develop our own candidate sentence selector.

[5]MEAD: http://www.summarization.com/mead

4.1 Evaluation of Content

4.1.1 Automatic Evaluation of Content

First, we have automatically evaluated the summaries generated by our approach for content. As a baseline, we used the original ranked list of candidate sentences (OList), and compared them to the final summaries (BlogSum). We have used the data from the TAC 2008 opinion summarization track for the evaluation.

The dataset consists of 50 questions on 28 topics; on each topic one or two questions are asked and 9 to 39 relevant documents are given. For each question, one summary was generated by OList and one by BlogSum and the maximum summary length was restricted to 250 words. This length was chosen cause in the DUC conference from 2005 to 2007, in the main summarization task, the summary length was 250 words. In addition, (Conroy and Schlesinger, 2008) also created summaries of length 250 words in their participation in the TAC 2008 opinion summarization task and performed well. (Conroy and Schlesinger, 2008) also pointed out that if the summaries were too long this adversely affected their scores. Moreover, according to the same authors shorter summaries are easier to read. Based on these observations, we have restricted the maximum summary length to 250 words. However, in the TAC 2008 opinion summarization track, the allowable summary length is very long (the number of non-whitespace characters in the summary must not exceed 7000 times the number of questions for the target of the summary). In this experiment, we used the ROUGE metric using answer nuggets (provided by TAC), which had been created to evaluate participants' summaries at TAC, as gold standard summaries. F-scores are calculated for BlogSum and OList using ROUGE-2 and ROUGE-SU4. In this experiment, ROUGE scores are also calculated for all 36 submissions in the TAC 2008 opinion summarization track.

The evaluation results are shown in Table 4. Note that in the table *Rank* refers to the rank of the system compared to the other 36 systems.

Table 4 shows that BlogSum achieved a better F-Measure (F) for ROUGE-2 (R-2) and ROUGE-SU4 (R-SU4) compared to OList. From the results, we can see that BlogSum gained 18% and 16% in F-Measure over OList using ROUGE-2 and ROUGE-SU4, respectively.

Table 4: Automatic Evaluation of BlogSum based on Summary Content on TAC 2008

System	R-2 (F)	R-SU4 (F)	Rank
Best	0.130	0.139	1
BlogSum	0.125	0.128	3
OList	0.102	0.107	10
Average	0.069	0.086	N/A

Compared to the other systems that participated to the TAC 2008 opinion summarization track, BlogSum performed very competitively; it ranked third and its F-Measure score difference from the best system is very small. Both BlogSum and OList performed better than the average systems.

However, a further analysis of the results of Table 4 shows that there is no significant difference between BlogSum-generated summaries and OList summaries using the t-test with a *p-value* of 0.228 and 0.464 for ROUGE-2 and ROUGE-SU4, respectively. This is inline with (Conroy and Schlesinger, 2008; Dang and Owczarzak, 2008) who showed that the performance gap between human-generated summaries and system-generated summaries at DUC and TAC is clearly visible in a manual evaluation, but is often not reflected in automated evaluations using ROUGE scores. Based on these findings, we suspected that there might be a performance difference between BlogSum-generated summaries and OList which is not reflected in ROUGE scores. To verify our suspicion, we have conducted manual evaluations for content.

4.1.2 Manual Evaluation of Content using the Blog Dataset

We have conducted two manual evaluations using two different datasets to better quantify BlogSum-generated summary content.

Corpora and Experimental Design

In the first evaluation, we have again used the TAC 2008 opinion summarization track data. For each question, one summary was generated by OList and one by BlogSum and the maximum summary length was again restricted to 250 words. To evaluate content, 3 participants manually rated 50 summaries from OList and 50 summaries from BlogSum using a blind evaluation. These summaries were rated on a likert scale of 1 to 5 where 1 refers to "very poor" and 5 refers to "very good". Evaluators rated each summary with respect to the question for which it was generated and against the reference summary. In this experiment, we have used the answer nuggets provided by TAC as the reference summary, which had been created to evaluate participants' summaries at TAC. Annotators were asked to evaluate summaries based on their content without considering their linguistic qualities.

Results

In this evaluation, we have calculated the average scores of all 3 annotators' ratings to a particular question to compute the score of BlogSum for a particular question. Table 5 shows the performance comparison between BlogSum and OList. The results show that 58% of the time BlogSum summaries were rated better than OList summaries which implies that 58% of the time, our approach has improved the question relevance compared to that of the original candidate list (OList).

Table 5: Comparison of OList and BlogSum based on the Manual Evaluation of Summary Content on TAC 2008

Comparison	%
BlogSum Score > OList Score	58%
BlogSum Score = OList Score	30%
BlogSum Score < OList Score	12%

Table 6 shows the performance of BlogSum versus OList on each likert scale; where Δ shows the difference in performance. Table 6 demonstrates that 52% of the times, BlogSum summaries were rated as "very good" or "good", 26% of the times they were rated as "barely acceptable" and 22% of the times they were rated as "poor" or "very poor". From Table 6, we can also see that BlogSum outperformed OList in the scale of "very good" and "good" by 8% and 22%, respectively; and improved the performance in "barely acceptable", "poor", and "very poor" categories by 12%, 8%, and 10%, respectively.

In this evaluation, we have also calculated whether there is any performance gap between BlogSum and OList. The t-test results show that in a two-tailed test, BlogSum performed significantly better than OList with a p-value of 0.00281.

Table 6: Manual Evaluation of BlogSum and OList based on Summary Content on TAC 2008

Category	OList	BlogSum	Δ
Very Good	6%	14%	8%
Good	16%	38%	22%
Barely Acceptable	38%	26%	-12%
Poor	26%	18%	-8%
Very Poor	14%	4%	-10%

Whenever human performance is computed by more than one person, it is important to compute inter-annotator agreement. This ensures that the agreement between annotators did not simply occur by chance. In this experiment, we have also calculated the inter-annotator agreement using Cohen's kappa coefficient to verify the annotation subjectivity. We have found that the average pair-wise inter-annotator agreement is moderate according to (Landis and Koch, 1977) with the kappa-value of 0.58.

4.1.3 Manual Evaluation of Content using the Review Dataset

We have conducted a second evaluation using the OpinRank dataset[6] and (Jindal and Liu, 2008)'s dataset to evaluate BlogSum-generated summary content.

Corpora and Experimental Design

In this second evaluation, we have used a subset of the OpinRank dataset and (Jindal and Liu, 2008)'s dataset. The OpinRank dataset contains reviews on cars and hotels collected from Tripadvisor (about 259,000 reviews) and Edmunds (about 42,230 reviews). The OpinRank dataset contains 42,230 reviews on cars for different model-years and 259,000 reviews on different hotels in 10 different cities. For this dataset, we created a total of 21 questions including 12 reason questions and 9 suggestions. For each question, 1500 to 2500 reviews were provided

[6]OpinRank Dataset: http://kavita-ganesan.com/entity-ranking-data

as input documents to create the summary.

(Jindal and Liu, 2008)'s dataset consists of 905 comparison and 4985 non-comparison sentences. Four human annotators labeled these data manually. This dataset consists of reviews, forum, and news articles on different topics from different sources. We have created 9 comparison questions for this dataset. For each question, 700 to 1900 reviews were provided as input documents to create the summary.

For each question, one summary was generated by OList and one by BlogSum and the maximum summary length was restricted to 250 words again. To evaluate question relevance, 3 participants manually rated 30 summaries from OList and 30 summaries from BlogSum using a blind evaluation. These summaries were again rated on a likert scale of 1 to 5. Evaluators rated each summary with respect to the question for which it was generated.

Results

Table 7 shows the performance comparison between BlogSum and OList. The results show that 67% of the time BlogSum summaries were rated better than OList summaries. The table also shows that 30% of the time both approaches performed equally well and 3% of the time BlogSum was weaker than OList.

Table 7: Comparison of OList and BlogSum based on the Manual Evaluation of Summary Content on the Review Dataset

Comparison	%
BlogSum Score > OList Score	67%
BlogSum Score = OList Score	30%
BlogSum Score < OList Score	3%

Table 8 demonstrates that 44% of the time BlogSum summaries were rated as "very good", 33% of the time rated as "good", 13% of the time they were rated as "barely acceptable" and 10% of the time they were rated as "poor" or "very poor". From Table 8, we can also see that BlogSum outperformed OList in the scale of "very good" by 34% and improved the performance in "poor" and "very poor" categories by 23% and 10%, respectively.

In this evaluation, we have also calculated whether there is any performance gap between BlogSum and OList. The t-test results show that in a two-tailed test, BlogSum performed significantly very better than OList with a p-value of 0.00236. In addition, the average pair-wise inter-annotator agreement is substantial according to (Landis and Koch, 1977) with the kappa-value of 0.77.

Table 8: Manual Evaluation of BlogSum and OList based on Summary Content on the Review Dataset

Category	OList	BlogSum	Δ
Very Good	10%	44%	34%
Good	37%	33%	-4%
Barely Acceptable	10%	13%	3%
Poor	23%	0%	-23%
Very Poor	20%	10%	-10%

4.1.4 Analysis

In both manual evaluation for content, BlogSum performed significantly better than OList. We can see that even though there was not any significant performance gap between BlogSum and OList-generated summaries in the automatic evaluation of Section 4.1.1, both manual evaluations show that BlogSum and OList-generated summaries significantly vary at the content level. For content, our results support (Conroy and Schlesinger, 2008; Dang and Owczarzak, 2008)'s findings and points out for a better automated summary evaluation tool.

4.2 Evaluation of Linguistic Quality

Our next experiments were geared at evaluating the linguistic quality of our summaries.

4.2.1 Automatic Evaluation of Linguistic Quality

To test the linguistic qualities, we did not use an automatic evaluation because (Blair-Goldensohn and McKeown, 2006) found that the ordering of content within the summaries is an aspect which is not evaluated by ROUGE. Moreover, in the TAC 2008 opinion summarization track, on each topic, answer snippets were provided which had been used as summarization content units (SCUs) in pyramid evaluation to evaluate TAC 2008 participants summaries but no complete summaries is provided to which we can compare BlogSum-generated summaries for coherence. As a result, we only performed two manual evaluations using two different datasets again to see whether BlogSum performs significantly better than OList for linguistic qualities too. The positive results of the next experiments will ensure that BlogSum-generated summaries are really significantly better than OList summaries.

4.2.2 Manual Evaluation of Discourse Coherence using the Blog Dataset

In this evaluation, we have again used the TAC 2008 opinion summarization track data. For each question, one summary was generated by OList and one by BlogSum and the maximum summary length was restricted to 250 words again. Four participants manually rated 50 summaries from OList and 50 summaries from BlogSum for coherence. These summaries were again rated on a likert scale of 1 to 5.

Results

To compute the score of BlogSum for a particular question, we calculated the average scores of all annotators' ratings to that question. Table 9 shows the performance comparison between BlogSum and OList. We can see that 52% of the time BlogSum summaries were rated better than OList summaries; 30% of the time both performed equally well; and 18% of the time BlogSum was weaker than OList. This means that 52% of the time, our approach has improved the coherence compared to that of the original candidate list (OList).

Table 9: Comparison of OList and BlogSum based on the Manual Evaluation of Discourse Coherence on TAC 2008

Comparison	%
BlogSum Score > OList Score	52%
BlogSum Score = OList Score	30%
BlogSum Score < OList Score	18%

From Table 10, we can see that BlogSum outperformed OList in the scale of "very good" and "good" by 16% and 8%, respectively; and improved the performance in "barely acceptable" and "poor" categories by 12% and 14%, respectively.

The *t*-test results show that in a two-tailed test, BlogSum performed significantly better than OList with a *p*-value of 0.0223. In addition, the average pair-wise inter-annotator agreement is substantial according to with the kappa-value of 0.76.

Table 10: Manual Evaluation of BlogSum and OList based on Discourse Coherence on TAC 2008

Category	OList	BlogSum	Δ
Very Good	8%	24%	16%
Good	22%	30%	8%
Barely Acceptable	36%	24%	-12%
Poor	22%	8%	-14%
Very Poor	12%	14%	2%

4.2.3 Manual Evaluation of Discourse Coherence using the Review Dataset

In this evaluation, we have again used the OpinRank dataset and (Jindal and Liu, 2008)'s dataset to conduct the second evaluation of content. In this evaluation, for each question, one summary was generated by OList and one by BlogSum and the maximum summary length was restricted to 250 words. Three participants manually rated 30 summaries from OList and 30 summaries from BlogSum for coherence.

Results

To compute the score of BlogSum for a particular question, we calculated the average scores of all annotators' ratings to that question. Table 11 shows the performance comparison between BlogSum and OList. We can see that 57% of the time BlogSum summaries were rated better than OList summaries; 20% of the time both performed equally well; and 23% of the time BlogSum was weaker than OList.

Table 11: Comparison of OList and BlogSum based on the Manual Evaluation of Discourse Coherence on the Review Dataset

Comparison	%
BlogSum Score > OList Score	57%
BlogSum Score = OList Score	20%
BlogSum Score < OList Score	23%

Table 12: Manual Evaluation of BlogSum and OList based on Discourse Coherence on the Review Dataset

Category	OList	BlogSum	Δ
Very Good	13%	23%	10%
Good	27%	43%	16%
Barely Acceptable	27%	17%	-10%
Poor	10%	10%	0%
Very Poor	23%	7%	-16%

From Table 12, we can see that BlogSum outperformed OList in the scale of "very good" and "good" by 10% and 16%, respectively; and improved the performance in "barely acceptable" and "very poor" categories by 10% and 16%, respectively.

We have also evaluated if the difference in performance between BlogSum and OList was statistically significant. The t-test results show that in a two-tailed test, BlogSum performed significantly better than OList with a p-value of 0.0371.

In this experiment, we also calculated the inter-annotator agreement using Cohen's kappa coefficient. We have found that the average pair-wise inter-annotator agreement is substantial according to (Landis and Koch, 1977) with the kappa-value of 0.74.

The results of both manual evaluations of discourse coherence also show that BlogSum performs significantly better than OList.

5 Conclusion

Based on the DUC and TAC evaluation results, (Conroy and Schlesinger, 2008; Dang and Owczarzak, 2008) showed that the performance gap between human-generated summaries and system-generated summaries, which is clearly visible in the manual evaluation, is often not reflected in automated evaluations using ROUGE scores. In our content evaluation, we have used the automated measure ROUGE (ROUGE-2 & ROUGE-SU4) and the t-test results showed that there was no significant difference between BlogSum-generated summaries and OList summaries with a *p-value* of 0.228 and 0.464 for ROUGE-2 and ROUGE-SU4, respectively. We suspected that there might be a performance difference between BlogSum-generated summaries and OList which is not reflected in ROUGE scores. To verify our suspicion, we have conducted two manual evaluations for content using two different datasets. The t-test results for both datasets show that in a two-tailed test, BlogSum performed significantly better than OList with a p-value of 0.00281 and 0.00236. Manual evaluations of coherence also show that BlogSum performs significantly better than OList. Even though there was no significant performance gap between BlogSum and OList-generated summaries in the automatic evaluation, the manual evaluation results clearly show that BlogSum-generated summaries are better than OList significantly. Our results supports (Conroy and Schlesinger, 2008; Dang and Owczarzak, 2008)'s findings and points out for a better automated summary evaluation tool.

Acknowledgement

The authors would like to thank the anonymous referees for their valuable comments on a previous version of the paper.

This work was financially supported by NSERC.

References

Annie Louis and Ani Nenkova. 2008. *Automatic Summary Evaluation without Human Models.* Proceedings of the First Text Analysis Conference (TAC 2008), Gaithersburg, Maryland (USA), November.

Chin-Y. Lin. 2004. *ROUGE: A Package for Automatic Evaluation of Summaries.* Text Summarization Branches Out: Proceedings of the ACL-04 Workshop, pages 74–81, Barcelona, Spain, July.

Dipanjan Das and Andre F. T. Martins. 2007. *A Survey on Automatic Text Summarization.* Available from: http://www.cs.cmu.edu/∼ nasmith/LS2/ dasmartins.07.pdf, Literature Survey for the Language and Statistics II course at Carnegie Mellon University.

Dragomir Radev et al. 2004. *MEAD -A Platform for Multidocument Multilingual Text Summarization.* Proceedings of the the 4th International Conference on Language Resources and Evaluation, pages 1–4, Lisbon, Portugal.

Hoa T. Dang and Karolina Owczarzak. 2008. *Overview of the TAC 2008 Update Summarization Task.* Proceedings of the Text Analysis Conference, Gaithersburg, Maryland (USA), November.

John M. Conroy and Judith D. Schlesinger. 2008. *CLASSY and TAC 2008 Metrics.* Proceedings of the

Text Analysis Conference, Gaithersburg, Maryland (USA), November.

John M. Conroy and Hoa T. Dang. 2008. *Mind the Gap: Dangers of Divorcing Evaluations of Summary Content from Linguistic Quality.* Proceedings of the the 22nd International Conference on Computational Linguistics Coling, pages 145–152, Manchester, UK.

Nitin Jindal and Bing Liu. 2006. *Identifying Comparative Sentences in Text Documents.* SIGIR'06 Proceedings of the 29th Annual International ACM SIGIR Conference on Research and Development in Information Retrieval, pages 244–251, Seattle, Washington, USA, August.

Richard J. Landis and Gary G. Koch. 1977. *A One-way Components of Variance Model for Categorical Data. Journal of Biometrics*, 33(1):671–679.

Sasha Blair-Goldensohn and Kathleen McKeown. 2006. *Integrating Rhetorical-Semantic Relation Models for Query-Focused Summarization.* Proceedings of the Document Understanding Conference (DUC) Workshop at NAACL-HLT 2006, New York, USA, June.

Shamima Mithun and Leila Kosseim. 2011. *Discourse Structures to Reduce Discourse Incoherence in Blog Summarization.* Proceedings of Recent Advances in Natural Language Processing, pages 479–486, Hissar, Bulgaria, September.

Author Index

Association for Computational Linguistics
209 N. Eighth Street
Stroudsburg, Pennsylvania 18360

CURRAN ASSOCIATES INC
proceedings.com